Tales Beyond the Dugout

"The zany antics of baseball players of the fifties"

By Ralph Mauriello

Dedicated to my wife June and our three daughters; Tami, Gina and Michelle.

FOREWARD

I pitched professional baseball for eight years a long time ago -1953-60 to be exact. I signed with the Brooklyn Dodgers in August, 1952 and spent eight years in their organization. I even had a chance to pitch in the big leagues -three games for the Dodgers their first year in Los Angeles in 1958.

In 1952, I was selected as a representative of the city of Los Angeles to play a high school All-Star game in New York City. After the game, I was asked to workout with the Yankees and the Dodgers. Since I was born and raised in Brooklyn (until I was 14), the Dodgers invitation was the most important.

After several workouts at Ebbets Field, I was invited to the main office where I met Walter O'Malley, who was then President of the Dodgers. I also met Fresco Thompson, then Vice President of Minor League Operations. After a short negotiation, we agreed on a $35,000 bonus and a $300 per month contract for Elmira New York, a Class A farm team of the Dodgers.

My career lasted 8 seasons and included a large number of minor league cities: Newport News, VA; Santa Barbara, CA; Pueblo, CO; Asheville, NC; Mobile, AL; St. Paul, MN (American Association); Fort Worth, TX; Victoria, TX; Los Angeles, CA (Pacific Coast League); Spokane, WA; and finally Montreal, Canada (International League) where I finished my career in 1960.

I've always told stories about my experiences as a professional baseball player. Recently my wife and daughters convinced me that I should write them down. This book is the result of their urging.

This book differs from most on baseball because it's not so much about the happenings on the field—although there is some of that—but more about the people that I encountered playing the game.

Some of them are famous, like Hall of Famers Don Drysdale, Sparky Anderson and Tommy Lasorda, and Dodger executives Walter O'Malley and Buzzie Bavasi. There's also a chapter on the game in Havana, Cuba, immediately after Fidel Castro took control of Cuba.

The book takes a look at the game then and now, and of course, pays homage to baseball fans.

So pull up a chair and let me tell you about some wild and crazy guys.

ACKNOWLEDGMENTS

My thanks to the people that made this book possible.

First, and foremost, to my wife June, and my three daughters, Tami, Gina and Michelle. June came up with the title, proof read, and made countless corrections. The girls reminded me of stories I had told them through the years, but had forgotten.

To my sister, Marjorie Mauriello Baker, a published author, who also provided guidance and editing skills.

To Gaylon White who was my mentor, providing valuable guidance throughout the process. He edited two chapters, suggested an additional chapter on singing, provided publishing contacts and finally coached me regarding preparation of a package for submission to potential publishers. He is the author of two baseball books, "The Bilko Athletic Club" and "Accidental Big Leaguer—Ransom Jackson".

To Joe Hoppel, a diehard Chicago Cubs fan, who lives in St. Louis. He reviewed my manuscript and caught several historic errors. He not only offered support and comments, but gave me a score card from Wrigley Field, Chicago, for the day of my only major league win. It's framed and hanging in my office.

Finally, thanks to my many enthusiastic supporters, who read the manuscript during its writing—including Jerry Reuss, ex-pitcher for the Dodgers, and particularly Stephanie and Murray MacLeod, who not only encouraged me to continue, but eagerly sought the next chapter.

Tales Beyond the Dugout

Table of Contents

Chapter 1 Ted Williams

He Wouldn't Sign a Kid's Autograph Book

You've probably heard that Ted Williams was a jerk. I'm here to tell you that's the truth.

The best example I can give you about this man's personality is the experience I had as a 12-year-old boy. At that time, (it was 1946) the Red Sox were being touted as perhaps one of the best teams in the history of baseball. Although I was a Brooklyn Dodgers fan, I was also a good baseball fan.

So I decided to get the autographs of every player on the team. The best way to do that was to go to the hotel that the Red Sox stayed at when they came to New York; I think it was the New Yorker Hotel.

I stood just outside the revolving door that led to the lobby, so I could ask for an autograph as the ballplayers came out. Several of the players did come out and I did get some autographs.

And then I really got lucky, I thought, because Ted Williams walked out the door. There were about seven or eight other kids also there at the Hotel New Yorker trying to get autographs of the Boston Red Sox. So it wasn't a surprise that he walked by us and said "Don't have time kids".

Three or four of us were not going to be put off that easily, so we followed him a few steps behind. We were hoping that he would stop at some point and sign our autographs because after all, there were only three or four of us. But he didn't stop.

It turned out I was the most persistent of the bunch, and after a while I was the only one following him. I walked behind him hoping for an opportunity. Then I got one. It was a red light and he couldn't cross the street.

I walked up to him and said "Mr. Williams while you're waiting for the light, would you please sign my autograph book."

And he said "Go away kid."

And when the light turned green, he walked across the street.

Well the story gets better. At about 4 o'clock, the bus that was used to take the Red Sox to the Yankee Stadium pulled up even with the lobby door, and the ballplayers started coming out.

One of the first ones to come out was the centerfielder, Dom DiMaggio. I asked him for an autograph and he stopped and signed my autograph book. Then he flipped through the pages and saw that I only had the autographs of three or four of his teammates.

He asked me "How long have you been here kid?"

I told him that I had been there since about noon.

He said "Wow, You haven't done very well. Let me take your book with me on the bus and I'll get all the guys to sign it."

You can imagine how excited I was as I watched each of the ballplayers getting on the bus. And I really was excited when I saw Ted Williams get onto the bus. I rubbed my hands with glee thinking that I was going to get the autograph of one of the best ballplayers in the history of the game.

As the bus started to pull out Dom DiMaggio leaned out the window and tossed my book and my pen toward me. I started flipping through the pages anxiously looking for Ted Williams autograph.

The jerk refused to sign . . . even while sitting on the bus waiting for it to take the team to Yankee Stadium.

That's my definition of a jerk.

Teddy Gives a Hitting Lecture

That being said I have to point out that he was probably the most respected ballplayer on the subject of hitting in the game of baseball. I say that because years later (1956), I was with the Dodgers during spring training and we were scheduled to play an exhibition game against the Red Sox.

I was sitting in the clubhouse after finishing my wind sprints. For those of you who don't know what wind sprints are . . . you run as hard as you can for about 60 yards and then turn around and walk back. . . . fast. You do this over and over for about 20 minutes. Yeah, it's exhausting.

After doing my wind sprints in the hot Miami sun, I was sitting in front of my locker, dripping with sweat. Now as you might expect, being a rookie, I had a locker right next to the door that led to the runway out to the dugout.

I was sitting there just dripping with sweat, when I heard somebody running in spike shoes on that concrete runway.

I thought what kind of a nut would be running on concrete in spikes. Probably some dumb rookie. You could really get hurt.

Was I surprised. It was Carl Erskine. Yeah that Carl Erskine ... the one who had already pitched the first of his two no-hitters.

He popped his head in the door and yelled "Hey guys. Teddy is taking batting practice."

The word was out that Williams was injured and probably wouldn't play that day. So I thought this was interesting, but I was really amazed at the reaction in the clubhouse.

Duke Snider, Gil Hodges, Pee Wee Reese, Carl Furillo, Roy Campanella . . . every one of the Boys of Summer . . . these guys who tore down the fences for the Dodgers for years, all got up and went out to see Ted Williams take batting practice. That's a sign of true respect.

Ted Williams;
Courtesy of the
Boston Red Sox

After Teddy finished taking his swings, the Dodger hitters backed him up against the grandstand behind home plate and started asking questions about his hitting techniques. Well, Teddy obliged and gave a lecture.

His hitting strategy was simple . . . for him. He just refused to swing at a pitch if it wasn't what he was looking for . . . unless he had two strikes. Then he would swing, but only if it was a strike.

4

So if he was looking for a fast ball and a pitcher threw a curve for a strike, he wouldn't swing unless he had two strikes. Or if he was looking inside and the pitch was outside, and he had less than two strikes he wouldn't swing.

So in essence his philosophy was to give the pitcher two strikes if necessary before he was willing to take his bat off the shoulder. While this strategy worked great for him, because of his great skills, most hitters couldn't afford that luxury.

Anyway that was his strategy.

I Get Even

As luck would have it, later that day, I found myself in the ball game with a man on base, and Ted Williams came in to pinch-hit.

I remembered what he had said, so I decided that I would start him with the fastball outside. I mean outside, not over the outside part of the plate, which he took for a ball. Next, I threw a curve ball right down the middle of the plate for a strike.

I still figured he was looking for a fastball over the plate, so I threw a fastball inside, which he took for ball. Then I threw another curve ball down the middle for a strike.

Now the count was two and two, and I'm sure he was looking for a fastball. So I threw my fastball, again outside. Now the count was full.

As I said, his philosophy was to never swing at a pitch that wasn't a strike, which is why I was counting on him to take pitches that were out of the strike zone. And that he would also take a pitch in the strike zone if it wasn't what he was looking for.

So with the count three and two, I was certain he was looking for fastball. So I threw a curve ball right down the middle. At the last moment, he flicked the bat out and hit a weak pop up to the shortstop for the out.

Well, the best part of the story is that was the end of the inning, and when we went into the dugout, Norm Larker, who was playing first base at the time, told me:

"Ralph, when you write your book you gotta put this in." (I don't know why he thought I would write a book, but it turns out he was right).

When I said "What do you mean?"

He said, "Teddy came down the first base line yelling 'What does that #$*&@ing rookie think this is #$*&@ing October? Throwing a three and two curve ball in Spring Training.'"

(You can figure out what the #$*&@ really was, the baseball players favorite "F" word).

So after many years you could say that I got my revenge against Ted Williams for being a mean jerk when I was a kid. He had refused to sign my autograph book while sitting in the bus with nothing to do.

Chapter 2 Don Drysdale

They Called Him "Porky"

The first time I remember seeing Don Drysdale was when I was in high school. He was in the 10th grade and I was in the 12th grade (a senior). I played for North Hollywood High and he played for our hated rival, Van Nuys High.

I was a pitcher and he was a second baseman. That's right! He played second base. And in case you remember the 6 foot, five inch pitcher with the Dodgers, you're going to be surprised to learn that as a 10th grader in high school, Don was five feet four inches tall, and more interesting . . his teammates called him Porky. That's right "Porky" Drysdale.

Don was batting seventh in the lineup. On one of my pitches, he deliberately pushed his bat back so he could hit the catcher's glove and claim catcher interference on his swing, and the umpire fell for it. So Don was awarded first base.

Now normally that's not the kind of incident that you would remember 60 years later . . . except that it turns out the next batter hit a home run.

Oh and did I mention that this was the bottom of the last inning and so we lost the game 3 to 2. It was one of only two games that I lost in my entire high school career. That's why I remember when I first saw Don Drysdale.

The next time I saw him was at a local park in North Hollywood in January or February of 1954. We had a lot of guys from our high school, nine to be exact, who had signed professional contracts during my three years in high school.

In fact, one of those guys was Bert Convy, who went on to be a fine stage and screen performer and popular TV game-show host. He was our first baseman. Good glove and good hit . . . for high school. He didn't go far in pro ball. He played parts of two seasons and then "hung 'em up."

Anyway, we would gather at the park to get ready for spring training. I was on the mound getting ready to pitch some batting practice, and I just happened to look down the right-field line and there was this big tall guy warming up with a catcher.

I asked Goldie Holt, who was a scout for the Dodgers at the time, "Who's that throwing down there?"

Goldie said "That's Drysdale."

And I said "I didn't know Don had an older brother,"

Goldie said "No, that's Don."

I just couldn't believe it. How could anybody grow that fast? In two years he had grown over a foot, become a pitcher, and he already had that nasty side arm delivery.

On the Field He Was Mean

I don't know what you've heard about Don over the years, but of course you've heard that he was a great competitor.

But he was really like Dr. Jekyll and Mr. Hyde. On the field he was one of the most competitive, and frankly, meanest guy you ever wanted to see. Off the field he really was a very nice guy.

How mean was he? Well we all know that in the era that Don and I pitched, the knockdown was the standard operating procedure. In fact, Don was famous throughout his career for knocking hitters down.

But maybe he went over the top one winter. We were playing in a league that was organized by the big-league clubs to give minor league ballplayers an opportunity to play in a competitive environment during the wintertime.

The Giants, the Dodgers, the Red Sox and the Indians, had teams in this league. We had at least six, maybe eight teams in the league, but I don't remember the other major league teams that sponsored ball clubs in that winter league.

I should remind everybody that we were living in Southern California where baseball was possible all year round. All the teams in the league were composed of professional minor league baseball players.

As luck would have it, the Dodgers juniors, as we were called, got to the final game of the playoffs. I don't remember if we won the league or not, but we were involved in a set of playoff games to determine a champion.

It wasn't a lot of money, but if we did win the final playoff game, we would each get about 50 or 60 bucks a man. If we lost, it would be 25 or 30 bucks a man. So we were playing for money . . . sort of.

I pitched the first three innings and held the other team scoreless. Another minor leaguer in the Dodger system by the name of Don Kenway, pitched the next three scoreless innings. Finally Drysdale, who had just finished his first year of pro ball at Class C Bakersfield, pitched the last three innings.

Don pitched two scoreless innings to get us to the top of the ninth and somehow, I don't remember how, the bases became loaded. I forget whether Don gave up hits or walks, but in any event the bases were loaded with nobody out. Don started bearing down and struck out the next two hitters.

Then he got a no ball, two strike count on the next hitter. The guy was a right-handed hitter and Don with that threatening side arm delivery threw a side arm curve ball to the batter.

The batter's rear end went out (as it usually did when Don threw his sidearm curve ball) and he reached out and hit the ball off the end of the bat. It just got over the first baseman's head, bounced just inside the foul line and rolled into foul territory.

With two outs, of course everybody was running, and before we could get the ball in, three runs had scored and we were now losing three to two.

Remember, we were playing for what amounted to peanuts. Well I'm sure it wasn't the money, but it was Don's competitive spirit that took over. The next batter was hit with Don's best fastball in the thigh.

In the era of knockdowns, we were taught (yes, we were taught) to knock a hitter down and not hit him. If you just wanted to knock him down, you were taught to throw the ball at his head. On the other hand, if you really wanted to hit him, you would throw the ball about waist high and behind him.

That's what Don did. I couldn't believe that in a game where there was really nothing at stake, that Don would react that way. But as I said, he was mean.

While I'm on the subject of that winter baseball team, I must mention Lefty Phillips, who at the time was a Dodger scout, was our manager. (Lefty went on to be a big league manager for the Anaheim Angels).

Lefty kept trying to fix up Don with my girlfriend. She came to all our games, and lived in the same neighborhood as Lefty.

He kept telling her that I was a real "run around", with a girl in every city, whereas Don was quiet and the probably more reliable as a guy to think about seriously.

I'm certainly glad that she didn't listen to Lefty; because that's the girl I wound up marrying. And after three daughters, and over 50 years, I'm still married to her.

Really Mean

Let's get back to Don's meanness. Consider that in a spring training game I got a base hit off of him in one of those countless intra-squad games. I hit a line shot on an outside fastball (really a sinker that didn't sink) to right-field. I hit it so hard that the right fielder actually threw to first base and almost got me out. I was safe on a bang-bang play. Actually I was out. The ump missed the call.

I guess that hit annoyed Don, because the next time I came up, the first pitch was right at my head. In fact, Roseboro the catcher yelled "Lookout" just about the moment Don let go of the ball, so he knew it was coming.

Off the Field, A Nice Guy

I mentioned Don was Jekyll and Hyde and I just finished giving you a character assassination. Let me tell you about Don Drysdale, the nice guy.

When I arrived in the big leagues in 1958, Don was already an established star. Yet, after almost every road game he would come by my locker and say "Gil and I (Gil Hodges was his roommate) are going to get a bite to eat. Wanna join us?"

Or I might be sitting in the lobby of the hotel in the afternoon and Don would come by and say "Gil and I are going to a movie. Wanna go?"

And I should mention that after knocking me down in that spring training game, we went out that night together into the bustling town of Vero Beach. So he really was a nice guy off the field.

Supreme Confidence

The last thing I should mention is his supreme confidence. We ran into one another at a North Hollywood/Van Nuys football game in the fall of 1954. Don had just finished an unremarkable season at Class C Bakersfield. He was 8 wins - 5 losses. Yet when I asked him where he thought he would be pitching the next season, he said "Montreal." (Montreal was the Dodgers top AAA farm club).

I responded by saying "You mean you'll sign a Montreal contract." What I left unsaid was that he would likely be optioned to Class A or Class B.

He picked up on what I was implying, and said "No, I'll be pitching for them." AND HE WAS RIGHT!

The next year he went to Montreal and had a great start. He was 11 wins and five losses midway through the season, and then something apparently happened, because he wound up the season at 11 and 11.

The official story was that Don broke a bone in his right hand when the lid of the Coke machine accidentally came down on his pitching hand. He didn't tell anybody, and kept on pitching, losing six straight before he finally reported that he had a broken finger.

I heard a rumor that was totally different. I was told about it by my old roommate Glenn Mickens. Now the rest of this has to come under heading of hearsay because I wasn't there. I just have Glenn's word on this.

By the way, Glenn didn't smoke, didn't drink, and didn't swear in the dugout like the rest of us. So you can draw your own conclusions.

According to Glenn, who was Don's teammate at Montreal during the 1955 season, he heard that Don was having a beer after one of the games, and this guy next to him asked Don where he was from.

When Don said he was from California, this guy made some remark about "California being the land of fruits and nuts." Don punched him with his right hand and literally knocked the guy off the bar stool. And that's how Don broke the finger in his pitching hand.

Whether it's true or not, Don had a great spring training in 1956 with the Dodgers, went north with them to Brooklyn, and the rest is history

Chapter 3 Ray Hathaway

Now I know you're saying who is Ray Hathaway and why is a chapter devoted to him? Well Ray is important to me, because he taught me how to pitch.

A Third Baseman for a Manager

I never thought about it at the time, but after I had retired, I thought it was strange that the Dodgers sent me to a minor league team (Class B Newport News) where the manager was a third baseman, Stan Wasiak.

After all, they had given me a $35,000 bonus, yet they sent me to a team where the manager knew very little about pitching. He was a playing manager-third baseman.

By the way, if you're wondering why I was allowed to go to the minors, while Koufax was required to go to the Dodgers for two years, it's because during 1952, when I signed, the "bonus rule" requiring two years in the majors was not in effect. It was in effect when Koufax signed in 1954.

In fact, Wasiak knew so little about pitching, that the starting pitchers were on a seven-day rotation. This was back in the day when the standard for starting pitchers was to pitch every fourth day. Yes, we had a pitching staff with seven starters and one reliever.

Well, not exactly just one reliever. After all, if you're starting once every seven days, you'll wind up pitching in relief in some of the other games. I relieved seven times before Wasiak got a telephone call from the Dodgers front office saying that I was a starter, not a reliever.

So I guess they were watching, but I don't think they really had a plan, because in my second season, they sent me to a team where the manager was an ex-second baseman, who knew as much about pitching as my first manager. In those days they didn't have roving minor-league pitching coaches, so I was left to figure things out for myself.

Fortunately for me, I did so poorly during the start of my second season, which was at Pueblo, Colorado in the Class A Western League, that I was sent down in June to Class B Asheville, North Carolina in the Tri-State League. I say fortunately, because the manager there was an ex-big-league pitcher by the name of Ray Hathaway. He's the one who taught me how to pitch.

I'll never forget the first time I pitched at Asheville. Just before I went out to the mound, Ray said to me "You're going nine tonight."

I said "Well, that's the plan." (This was back when a pitcher was expected to finish the ball game.)

Ray answered by saying "You're going nine tonight. I don't care how many runs they get off you. I want to see you pitch."

As it turned out, I did finish the ball game--and won.

After the game, Ray said "Ralph you've got big league stuff, but there are three things keeping you out of the big leagues. We'll have to work on your follow-through, teach you a change up and you'll have to knock hitters down."

Fixing My Follow-through

First, he improved my follow-through, which helped in two ways. It made me a better fielder because I was in a better position to field the ball hit back at me, and probably more important, it improved my control. A key item in improving my follow-through was his demanding that I keep my eye on the catcher's glove even after I let go of the pitch.

I argued with him. I said "I want to keep my eye on the ball once I let it go, just in case somebody hit the ball back at me."

And he pointed out that if I didn't throw the ball so that it wound up in my line of vision, then the chances of the hitter hitting the ball were pretty small.

So I didn't have to worry about somebody hitting a line drive back at me. And of course if I did throw the ball in the strike zone, my eyes would pick it up and if the hitter did hit it back at me, I'd have no trouble fielding it. It felt funny at first but after I got the hang of it, it did improve my control quite a bit.

Learning the Change Up

Then we began to work on the change-up, which is designed to throw off the hitter's timing. Ray gave me a graphic demonstration of the value of the change up. Ray was in his late 30s, so he could still pitch and he often threw batting practice to the team.

Two or three days after I joined the team, he called me in from the outfield (that's where pitchers are supposed to be during batting practice) and said "Ralph I want you to stand behind the batting cage."

He started each hitter with fastballs, which is the usual approach in BP, and then after a few pitches, he would tell the hitter "Here comes a change."

And even though the hitters knew what was coming, they'd pop it up or beat it into the dirt, or sometimes miss it completely.

After he finished his demonstration, he came in and told me "That's the power of the change up. Even though they know it's coming, they have trouble hitting it. Imagine what it would be like if they don't know what's coming."

"When you learn how to throw a change up for a strike when the count is 2-0 or 3-1, you will be a pitcher. . . and not before."

He taught me the change up in the same way that I teach young kids the change up now. He told me that there are lots of ways to throw the change up, and that he would show me all of them. He asked me to try each of them, give each a fair trial, and then pick the one that I like the best.

Ray taught me how to throw the change up and he taught me well. I struck people out with the change up, and it's really designed to get the hitter off stride so that he hits a weak fly ball or ground ball.

The next season, when I was in Mobile I can't tell you how many times the count was 2-0 or 3-1, and sometimes 3-2 and I'd throw a change up for a strike and get an out.

After a lot of practice sessions, Ray thought that I was ready to use it in a game. He didn't tell me that he thought I was ready;

he just sprung it on me as I was walking out to the mound one night to start the game.

Ray said "Tonight we're going to work on the change up. I don't care how many runs they get off of you, you're going to throw the change up. I'll call the pitches from the dugout tonight, so don't shake off Ken." (Ken Worley was our catcher).

It was a nerve-racking night. I gave up a few runs, but I was able to use the change-up effectively, and we won the game.

A week later we're playing the same team, and Ray said to me "Ralph you got them all screwed up on the change up last week. So tonight I want you to throw nothing but fastballs the first time through the lineup. Ken is going to keep sticking down that number one finger until you get through the lineup one time."

He didn't care whether we won or lost the ball game. He was teaching me to pitch. So I went out there and threw nothing but fastballs . . . . and I got eight straight fly balls to center field, before I struck out the pitcher. I don't remember whether we won or lost the game, but I was taught a lesson by Ray.

After the game he said "Ralph you set up hitters from pitch to pitch, from at bat to at bat, and from game to game."

"Knock That Guy on His Ass."

Finally he taught me to knock down hitters. We had a debate over this. I refused to throw at a hitter. For one thing, I was afraid I might hurt somebody. For another thing, there was a very successful pitcher in the major leagues who refused to knock down hitters. Robin Roberts, who turned out to be a Hall of Famer, was the guy.

Of course, I should point out that Roberts also led the league in home runs allowed every year. That was part of Ray's reasoning for asking that I knock hitters down.

He said "You got to knock hitters down once in a while so they won't dig in on you."

He tried to convince me, but I just wouldn't do it.

Then there was the night when I pitched the opening game of a twilight doubleheader. Those games started in the twilight, after the sun went down, but before it was dark enough for the lights to take effect. So it was pretty tough to see the ball . . . especially the fastball.

For my entire career, whenever I faced the leadoff hitter, my strategy was simple. Throw the fastball down the middle and dare him to hit it.

Well I cranked up my best fastball, and it got away from me. I mean really got away from me and went right at the batter's head. He went down sprawled in the dirt.

No I didn't hit him. It was a classic knockdown . . . by accident.

I recovered my control and was able to get through the inning with three straight outs.

We were in the third base dugout, so as I walked off the mound, I passed Ray, who was going out to coach third base.

Ray said "Ralph, one pitch, three outs."

What he meant was that even though the first pitch was an accidental knockdown, they didn't know it, and it intimidated not only the first hitter, but the next two guys as well.

The next inning, I got three straight outs, and as I was walking back to the dugout, Ray, on his way to the third base coach's box, said, "Ralph, one pitch, six outs".

I pitched another inning, got three straight outs and as I was walking back to the dugout, Ray, on his way to the third base coach's box said "Ralph, one pitch, nine outs."

I got the first two outs in the fourth inning, before somebody got a single. After the inning, Ray said "Ralph, one pitch, 11 outs. You really need to think about the knock-down pitch."

Of course his point was that knocking down the first hitter made everybody a little nervous. In spite of that, I still refused to intentionally knock a hitter down.

Then one or two starts later, Spartanburg came to town with the league's leading hitter. We were playing in a four-game series and in the first three games he got seven or eight hits.

Just before I went out to pitch in the first inning, Ray in his colorful style said "Dammit Ralph, I want you to knock that guy on his ass."

I said "Ray you know we've been through this. I'm not gonna knock him down."

He said "Okay. How about if you throw your best fastball about 3 inches from his nose. I'm not asking you to throw at his head. Just throw close."

I said "Okay I can do that."

What I think Ray was counting on, was the fact that my control wasn't that good.

I threw my best fastball and aimed it about 3 inches from his nose, but the ball went right at his head. It didn't hit him, but he wound up sprawled in the dirt. And a funny thing . . . he wound up the most polite 0 for 4 that night that you ever saw.

That convinced me, that there's a time and a place for the knockdown. So from then on, I threw the knockdown when I thought it would help.

Now that I was convinced of the value of the knockdown, Ray continued his teaching.

"First of all" he said "you don't want to hit the guy, that'll put a runner on first. You want to intimidate him. The head is the most mobile part of the body, and the hitter has a very strong feeling of self-preservation. So he's gonna do whatever he can to get his head out of the way."

"But there's gonna be a time when you hafta hit a guy. If one of your guys gets hit with a pitch, you're gonna be expected to get even and hit one of their guys."

"You have to do that to protect your teammates. It's not going to happen very often, but you must know that if you want to hit a guy you don't throw at his head. You throw the ball about waist high and behind the hitter."

That's right, in my day, pitchers were not only taught how to knockdown hitters, but to hit a guy if needed, because it was considered a part of the game.

And there were unwritten rules.

You usually didn't knockdown a weak hitter. If a player hit a home run, it was a good bet that his next time up, the pitcher would throw a knock down--or certainly brush him back.

If you were the next hitter after someone hit a home run, there was a chance you might get knocked down. Not knowing whether or not you were a target prevented a lot of guys from digging in. And remember, this was all before we had the hard plastic helmets that we have today.

Knockdowns Were Truly a Part of the Game

Knockdowns were just part of the game. I can tell you a story to convince you.

I was still pitching in Asheville with Ray Hathaway as my manager, and we were in the playoffs against Greenville. It was early in the game and the Greenville centerfielder, Len Pecou, slid into our second baseman and cut him very badly on a force out with two down.

It might have been excusable if it was an attempt to break up a double play, but there were two out so there was no need to slide and cut up our second baseman. In fact, he cut him so badly, (it was a two or three inch gash) that our second baseman was forced out of the game.

Ray didn't need to tell me that the next time Pecou came up, the first pitch better be a knock-down. He went down in the dirt, and came up screaming at me and waving his bat. I couldn't hear a word he was saying, because it was a full house and the crowd was really screaming.

After all I had just knocked down their favorite ballplayer. He was hitting over .300 and batting third in the lineup.

So I figured I had done my job. Got even! I sent the message that we weren't going to put up with his attitude. I confess, I *was* tempted to hit him, but it was the playoffs, and I didn't want to put a guy on base in a close ballgame.

When I looked in to get the sign for my next pitch, I heard a whistle. We were in the first base dugout that night, and I looked over my left shoulder and there was Ray giving me a sign with his two hands to knock the hitter down.

He was doing this on the front step of the dugout. So everybody in the ballpark, including the umpires could see that I was being ordered to knock the hitter down.

On the next pitch, Pecou went down again. He came up screaming at me, and again I couldn't hear him. He was waving the bat at me like he was going to come out and get me. My thought was that my catcher will get him before he ever gets to me, so I wasn't too worried.

I looked in to get my sign for the next pitch and I heard a whistle. I turned around and there was Ray telling me to knock him down again. So I did. And he came up waving his bat and screaming. I still couldn't hear him.

Now the count was 3-0. I'm slow, but I'm not that slow. Instead of looking in to get my sign first, I turned around to look at our dugout. Ray was standing on the dugout steps, shrugging his shoulders as if to say go ahead and pitch to him.

I threw two fastballs for two strikes to get to 3-2, and then I walked him. I didn't want to. But I walked him. He trotted down to first, stepped on the bag, raised his hands and asked for time.

I figured that he was coming after me, so I threw my glove down and waited. But he didn't come after me. He went straight into our dugout and attacked Ray.

Ray kicked the hell out of him. He came out of the dugout bleeding from the nose and mouth. He was a bloody mess.

When I came back to the dugout after the inning was over, one of our pitchers told me that Ray was mad at all the guys on the bench because they didn't help him.

Another of our pitchers said that he told Ray "Hell Ray, if we helped you, he'd be dead."

Here's the payoff to this whole story. I didn't get thrown out of the game. Nor did Ray get thrown out of the game. The only guy who got thrown out, was the hitter . . . because he charged our dugout.

Yes, it was a very different culture then, than now.

The next season I was at Mobile in the AA Southern Association. I won 18 and lost eight, during the season, and added four more wins in the playoffs.

After we beat Memphis and Birmingham to become the Southern Association champions, we played and beat Shreveport, the Texas League Champions in the Dixie Series. (just like the World Series, only at the minor league AA level).

As added bonus, I won the Rookie of Year award in the Southern Association.

Yes, Ray taught me how to pitch!

.

Chapter 4 I Never Called Him Sparky

I never called George "Sparky" Anderson, Sparky. He was my teammate in 1957, when we were both with the LA Angels of the Pacific Coast League, and even though he got the nickname in '55, we all called him Georgie.

The reporters of the local papers also called him Georgie, whenever they mentioned him in a column or a story about the game.

Funny thing is, when I would call the house and Carol (his wife) answered, I would ask for Georgie, She'd say "Just a minute Ralph. I know it's you because you're the only one who calls him Georgie."

We Were Teammates

We were also teammates at Santa Barbara in 1953. He was the kind of a guy who was full of pep and energy. His enthusiasm was great.

He never seemed to get down on himself. He played shortstop that year, but he shifted to second base the next season, when he realized that his arm wasn't strong enough for shortstop.

The thing I remember most about that year was his zeal for wanting to score 100 runs, and he did it the last day in 1953; and he was very excited about it. But he paid a terrible price.

Like most ballplayers Georgie was superstitious. As we were getting near the end of the season, it looked like Georgie wasn't going to get his 100 runs scored. Then he had a big day when he scored three runs.

So he decided for good luck that he would not change or wash his jockstrap for the next game. . . and he scored a run. This went on for the last eight or nine days of the season. As I said, he did get his 100 runs scored, but he had the worst case of jock itch you ever saw.

While we were in Santa Barbara, Georgie and I stayed at the same home as four other guys on the team. We rented rooms in one of those big Santa Barbara homes that easily accommodated six of us.

We had three pitchers, a catcher and two infielders. Maybe you remember one of the other pitchers, George Witt, who spent some time in the majors with the Pittsburgh Pirates. The other infielder was our second baseman, Dale Johnson. Georgie also roomed with him on the road.

One time after a loss in San Jose, a bunch of us were out in the hall of the hotel, throwing water balloons at each other. Then Georgie and Dale decided to throw some water balloons out of their hotel window at the people below.

When somebody on the floor below stuck his head out, he got a water balloon thrown at him. Unfortunately for Georgie, that "head" belonged to our manager, George Scherger (Scherger was a coach for Georgie for many years in Cincinnati).

Scherger came upstairs and fined all of us. He was very unhappy . . . especially after a loss. Oh yeah, I was the starting and losing pitcher (I went 7 1/3 innings) that night. Scherger was especially mad at me.

Then there was the time when we were in Santa Barbara. Dale and I were coming home late one night after chasing some girls. After all, we were 19 and single. Georgie was also 19 and single, but he had already decided that he was going to marry Carol, so he never went out after the ball games.

Dale and I came home late (i.e. after curfew) and Dale got this crazy idea of testing an old theory that he had heard about. That was that if a guy is sleeping and you stick his hand in a bucket of water, he will pee in bed.

So Dale and I decided to test the theory. We filled the bucket with water, put it alongside of Georgie's bed, and moved his hand off the side of the bed so it went into the bucket. He woke up, but he didn't pee. Theory disproved.

In 1954, we were teammates in Pueblo Colorado. That was Class A. George Witt also was with us. As I mentioned earlier, Georgie moved to second base, so that it was possible for Maury Wills to play shortstop. Yeah that Maury Wills.

They made a great double-play combination and that year Georgie hit .260 and led the league in fielding at second base.

Georgie Always Looked Like an Old Man

Another interesting thing about Georgie was that when he was only 36 years old, he really looked like an old man.

When he was managing the Cincinnati Reds and they would do a close-up of him in the dugout, my wife would say "How old is he? He can't be the same age as you. Look at his hair, It's white."

So I told her this story about Georgie when we were working out at USC, trying to get in shape before the start of the '57 season. We were going to be teammates that year in the Pacific Coast League Los Angeles Angels.

I was in the outfield shagging fly balls during batting practice, and one of the USC varsity infielders came out to shag fly balls. We started talking and during the conversation he said how grateful he was that an old pro like Georgie would come out and workout with the SC team and show them some of the finer points of playing second base.

George "Sparky" Anderson, manager of the Cincinnati Reds at age 36; Courtesy Cincinnati Reds

I looked at him and said "How old do you think he is?"

And he responded with " 33 or 34".

When I told him that we (Georgie and I) were the same age . . 23, he said "No way."

I said "Oh yes he is. We played against each other when we were in high school."

The Great LA-Hollywood Riot

At least that's what they called it in the newspapers the next day. It was 1957, and the Los Angeles Angels were playing the Hollywood Stars, our bitter intra-city rivals, when one of those bench clearing "brawls" happened.

If you've seen enough of those brawls, you realize that most of the time two or three guys are really upset and throwing punches, while the rest of the guys are really kind of "waltzing" with one another.

In this particular case, the guys that were mad at one another were Tommy Lasorda (yeah, that Tommy Lasorda) of the Angels and "Spook" Jacobs of the Stars. They're the guys who started fighting and then both benches cleared.

Earlier in the Jacobs at bat, Tommy had knocked down Jacobs. Jacobs responded by doing what hitters often did when they got knocked down. They'd lay a bunt down the first base line with the intent of running up the pitcher's back when he tried to field the ball.

Jacobs laid a bunt down the first base line, but things didn't go according to his plan. Instead of trying to field the ball, Lasorda hit him with a flying tackle. Lasorda was actually parallel to the ground when he hit Jacobs in the waist. They started rolling around in the dirt and the benches cleared.

But as I said earlier, most of the other guys were trying to make believe they were fighting. The best example of that is that, while I was pushing some guy, no punches thrown, I looked over his shoulder and I saw "Sparky" Anderson with his head buried in the chest of George Witt, who was a pitcher for the Stars.

Witt was originally in the Dodger organization and was a good friend of both Georgie and I. So I was really surprised, because it looked like Georgie was really pounding Witt in the stomach.

I ran over there to see if maybe I could break them up, and I heard Georgie saying to Witt "Does this look okay? We want to put on a good show don't we?"

As I said two guys were really mad, and the rest of us were waltzing around the field. A little pushing and shoving but nobody threw a punch except Lasorda and Jacobs.

I guess the act that Georgie and Witt put on was bought by the members of the press, because the next day the headlines blared:

"RIOT AT GILMORE FIELD."

A Triple A Manager at 30

The most amazing thing was to run across Georgie in the off season between '63 - '64 seasons at the Forum in Inglewood, Calif. I was on my way to get a beer from the concession stand at halftime during a Laker basketball game when I bumped into Georgie.

He knew that I was out of baseball and asked me about what I was doing. I told him I was working as a computer design engineer for an aerospace company and was having a good time.

I also told him that since I retired from baseball, I had dropped my subscription to the Sporting News (a weekly newspaper dedicated to Baseball) and had no idea how he was doing. I told him that the last I had heard was that he was still playing second base for the Toronto Maple Leafs of the AAA International League.

Imagine how surprised I was when he told me that he was going to manage the Toronto ball club the next year. Managing at the AAA level when you're 30 years old is really quite an accomplishment.

He told me that the owner of the Toronto club, Jack Kent Cooke, had observed Georgie doing the kinds of things he always did. That was to help a lot of guys on the team with the different aspects of the game. He was sort of an unofficial coach. Cooke was so impressed that he offered Georgie the job to manage the ball club.

Litton Management Club

You've probably heard about Sparky's character and how much time he spent supporting charities. I have a story about Sparky that you might find interesting.

I was the entertainment chairman of the Litton Management Club, so it was my job to a find speakers or entertainment of some sort for our monthly meetings. So it seemed like a

natural to me to contact Georgie and ask him if he would speak at the Litton Management club.

When I called him, he said "A bunch of Engineers? That ought to be interesting."

George "Sparky" Anderson and me at Litton Management Club dinner in 1984; Author's collection

My problem was that I was sure his fee for speaking at dinners etc. might be a little more than we had in our budget. So I asked him what his fee was.

He said "Ralph, I don't think you can afford me. What do you have in your budget?"

I was a little embarrassed, but I said "$1200."

He said "Okay I'll do it for $1200, but when you write the check make it out to a charity in Detroit. I'll give you the name when the time comes."

Georgie lived in Thousand Oaks California, very close to California Lutheran University. Georgie not only sponsored an annual fund raising Golf tournament for the baseball program, but he also made several nice financial donations.

In 2006 California Lutheran University named their new baseball field George "Sparky" Anderson field to thank him for his support.

He was a great guy, a good team mate and a giver!

Chapter 5 Chuck Connors - The Rifleman

I met Chuck Connors when I was a senior in high school. It was 1952. He was playing for the AAA Los Angeles Angels in the old Pacific Coast League. Los Angeles had two teams in the league; the Angels and the Hollywood Stars.

Chuck Tells Me He's Gonna Be a Movie Star

I was a standout pitcher in high school, and in those days they didn't have a draft like they do now. So every high school graduate was a free agent, free to sign with any team.

So teams like the Angels and the Stars, which were farm clubs of the Pittsburgh Pirates and the Chicago Cubs, courted us prospects in whatever way they could. I could get free tickets to any of the games, and they invited me to pitch batting practice so I could get to know the guys.

One day I was standing in the outfield after pitching batting practice, and Chuck Connors came over to me and thanked me for the way I pitched batting practice.

He said "Kid you throw great batting practice. You understand that it's batting practice. You're not trying to get the hitter's out. You lay the ball in there so we can hit it."

I told him that I was taught that by my dad and he said "Oh your dad played pro ball."

I said "No, he's a barber, but he's a real student of the game."

We became friends I guess, because it seemed like every time I finished pitching batting practice and went to the outfield,

Chuck would come alongside me and we'd start talking about different things.

One night he told me how he knows all these Hollywood producers. He dropped a few names, and told me how when he retired from baseball, "I'm gonna become a movie star."

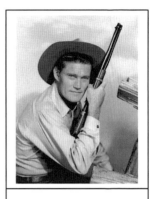

ABC Publicity still of Chuck Connors for The Rifleman

Now I was 18 years old and I didn't think it was my place to tell this 36-year-old man that the day after he retires from baseball, nobody is going to know who he is. So I just kept quiet and thought to myself 'This poor guy is deluded."

Well just imagine how surprised I was when in 1958 I was in Philadelphia with the Dodgers and was going to the movies with Don Drysdale and Gil Hodges. The movie was "The Big Country". I didn't pay much attention to who was in the movie but I do remember Gregory Peck was in it. But the big surprise was to look up and see Chuck Connors on the big screen.

He was right when he said "I'm going to be a movie star."

I'm sure you all remember him as the star of the old TV show, "The Rifleman"

Behind the Batting Cage

When Tommy Lasorda was managing the Dodgers, I often called him to get free tickets to the game. I'd arrive early and go down on the field and talk to Tommy behind the batting cage during batting practice.

One night while we were standing around talking about the game the night before, Chuck Connors, The Rifleman, showed up.

It turns out he and Tommy were teammates in the minor leagues and Tommy couldn't resist telling me stories about the crazy things that they did when they were playing ball together.

One story that I thought was particularly funny was how he and Chuck used to work it to get a free meal.

Tommy said "We would catch a cockroach and take it into the restaurant in a matchbox. We would order a meal and when we were almost finished, we'd would call the waitress over and show her that there was a cockroach on the plate. Of course, the manager always gave us a free meal."

I'm sure that they could only pull that once in each restaurant, but Tommy said they did it whenever they could, because you had to do something to stretch the meal money. It was never enough!

As the conversation went on, I reminded Chuck that when I was in high school I used to throw batting practice to the Angels when he was playing for them. After he took his swings he would come out to right-field where I was shagging fly balls.

I reminded him how he told me he was going to be a movie star. I couldn't resist telling him that when he was telling me about his dreams of being a movie star, I thought he was off his rocker. But it turned out just the way he said it would. He had a very successful career in the movies and television.

Dodgers Alumni Association

Chuck appeared in only one game for the Dodgers and I appeared in three games, but in spite of such a short stay in the bigs for us, we were both members of the Dodgers Alumni, which is an organization in name only. It certainly is an honor to be in the organization, but it has no purpose and does nothing.

One night while we were complaining about the fact that the organization was not doing anything worthwhile, we decided it would be a good idea to get the Dodger Alumni behind a fundraising event for a worthwhile charity. We kicked around some ideas like a tennis tournament or a golf tournament and then finally settled on a nationwide TV show.

The plan for a nationwide show was a natural because the Dodgers had alumni all over the country. We could put our alumni at the TV stations and have the people call in and pledge money to the charity for an opportunity to speak to their favorite ball player.

We had alumni all over the country; Clem Labine in New England, Carl Furillo in Pennsylvania, Carl Erskine in Indiana . . . well you get the idea. We could do a simulcast all over the country and raise money for a good charity.

So Chuck and I decided to approach Peter O'Malley, then the Dodgers owner, with the idea of using Dodger Alumni as the vehicle for fundraising for a charity he would choose.

We wrote a letter to Bill Shumard, Director of Community Services, asking him to pass on our idea to Mr. O'Malley, and arrange a meeting with him so we could discuss details.

BILL SHUMARD   DEC.2 1984
DODGER STADIUM
LOS ANGELES, CA.

Dear Bill,

As we agreed on Wednesday, I'm submitting my thoughts on potential Dodger Alumni activities. These thoughts as you will see are more in the form of an outline to guide us to an activity that is mutually beneficial to the community and the Dodgers.

I believe that some exploratory discussions with the outline below, used as a guide, would be the first step. Naturally, Mr. O'Malley's approval would be required. So he should be present to guide us down the path that he chooses.

1. I believe a philanthropic activity is probably the best way to find an activity that is mutually beneficial. Options are:

   a. Select a charity to support.
   b. Identify or create a new cause worthy of support.

2. The next question to be asked is : What type of involvement? The options are:

   a. Sponsor an event
   b. Sponsor and Participate in an event

3. Next, is who is involved? The obvious answer is Dodger Alumni; but just those local to the So. California area, or ALL Dodger alumni throughout the U.S. The answer to this question may definitely affect the other answers.

4. Finally, the question is what type of event? Some of the options are:

   a. A Game; Baseball, basketball, etc.
   b. A Tournament; Golf, Tennis, Etc
   c. A Telethon

Well that's the outline for your and Mr. O'Malley's consideration. Naturally, I believe that Chuck Connors and myself should be included in these exploratory discussions. Please call me as soon as you have had a chance to review the above material. We are very interested in your reaction.

Although both Chuck and I were sold on the idea of a nationwide telethon, as you read the letter, you can see we felt it best to provide options.

Peter O'Malley Says No

Mr. O'Malley did not respond to our letter, but several months later Chuck and I, along with lots of other Dodgers alumni and active players, were at a banquet in Beverly Hills honoring Rick Monday who had just retired.

Naturally, Mr. O'Malley was at the party and after the festivities were over, Chuck and I approached him regarding our proposal. I reminded Mr. O'Malley that we had sent him a letter suggesting that we use the Dodgers Alumni as means to raise money for a charity of his choice.

Since he hadn't responded to my letter, I asked if he had received it. He said he had, and had decided to take no action.

When I asked him why, he said (I'm paraphrasing here) "If you give money to one charity, then all the charities will come after you"

Now I'm sure Mr. O'Malley donates generously to various charities. I think he just didn't want to deal with a couple of wise guys.

I remember responding "Well isn't that the fun of having money. You get to do with it what you like."

He didn't like my smart aleck remark, kind of mumbled something, and walked off.

Chuck and I looked at one another, shrugged our shoulders and knew our idea was dead.

Chapter 6 Baseball Executives I Knew

Walter O'Malley - Dodgers Owner

Walter O'Malley owned and ran the Dodgers for almost 30 years. He's the guy who moved the Dodgers from Brooklyn to Los Angeles. Of course the people in Brooklyn never forgave him and accused him of greed. After all the Brooklyn franchise was very successful financially. But the fans of O'Malley in baseball, and in LA, thought he was a visionary.

By the way, he was elected to the Hall of Fame for his contributions to, and influence on, the game

Asking about LA in '55

I think he was a visionary; at least a very good long range planner. I'm sure you've heard or read about how Walter O'Malley was pushed out of Brooklyn by some guy named Robert Moses. Moses wouldn't approve of a new stadium that O'Malley wanted to have built in Brooklyn to replace the old Ebbets Field. By the way, O'Malley's plan called for a domed stadium; years before the Astrodome.

Moses wanted the new stadium to be built in Queens, where the New York Mets play now. O'Malley protested pointing out that the team was called the *Brooklyn* Dodgers and it made no sense for the park to be in Queens. Moses wouldn't give in, and O'Malley left town.

I'm not sure when those confrontations started taking place, but I can tell you that in spring training in 1955, I was sitting in the lobby of the Dodgertown facility in Vero Beach Florida, when Mr. Walter O'Malley came over and sat down next me.

Since he was there when I signed with the Dodgers, for a lot of money, he knew who I was, and I'm sure was keeping track of my progress through the minor leagues. For a while, it seemed he was interested in my progress in the minors.

But then out of a clear blue sky he said to me "You live in Los Angeles don't you? "

When I said "Yes", he started asking me questions about the people in Los Angeles and if they were good baseball fans.

I remember my response was something like "I know they love their football, but I'm not sure about baseball. All of my friends, of course, are very interested in baseball, but I don't think that's the general feeling in LA."

"I think that the football is king in Los Angeles, because the UCLA Bruins, the USC Trojans and the Los Angeles Rams can schedule three games in the same weekend, Friday night, Saturday and Sunday afternoons, and all the games will draw over 60,000 people."

"On the other hand the when I went to baseball games in the Pacific Coast League, and in LA we had two teams, the Hollywood Stars and the Los Angeles Angels, the crowds were seldom over 5,000."

So after a long-winded roundabout soliloquy, I finally told him that I thought LA was not a good baseball town. That was February, 1955.

I guess he was already doing long range planning. I know he didn't listen to me, because on October 8, 1957, the Dodgers announced that they were leaving Brooklyn and coming to Los Angeles.

"Buzzie" Bavasi - Dodgers General Manager

"Buzzie" Bavasi was the General Manager of the Dodgers from 1951 to 1968, so I had lots of interactions with him during the years that I was with the Dodgers. His job was to stock the ball club with talent, and then let the manager run the team on the field.

He must have done a very good job of picking the players, because during his time with the Dodgers, the team won eight National League pennants and its first four World Series titles.

Buzzie had a short temper, but was willing to listen. For instance, take the flap over night games in Spring Training.

Carl Furillo and Flap About Night Games

We were in Miami to play some exhibition games. One morning, as I was walking into the dining room of the McAllister Hotel, I saw Buzzie coming out.

He came toward me with fire in his eyes and said "All right! If you don't like night games in spring training, report to St. Paul clubhouse as soon as possible."

I was stunned and I said "What did I do now?"

He said "Take a look at this."

He showed me an article that had been cut out of the New York Times sports section, with a circle in red around it and handwriting saying "What's this? Walt"

I didn't have to be told that "Walt" was Walter O'Malley and he was upset at the article because the headlines said

"FURILLO, MAURIELLO BASH NIGHT SPRING BASEBALL."

Now I knew why Buzzie was upset. I said "Give me a chance to explain"

He said "OK! But you're wasting your time."

I explained how the story in the paper came about. A couple nights earlier, Carl Furillo and I were standing on the curb waiting for a taxi to take us to the ballpark.

By the way, Carl was one of the "Boys of Summer". He was the right fielder for the Dodgers during their glory years in the late 1940's and 50's. He played his entire 15-year career with the Dodgers. He had a career batting average of .299, with192 home runs and 1,058 runs batted in.

While we were standing there, a New York Times sports writer came driving by and said "Hey you guys want a lift?"

So we hopped in, and while we were going to the ballpark, Carl gave a long speech on night baseball and why it was bad in spring training. He pointed out that young guys like me who are trying to make the team might get hurt because the nights are cold and damp.

I said "Honest Buzzie, why would I complain about night ball. The lights are never as good as daylight. Night ball is an advantage for me. Besides, Carl did most of the talking. You know Carl. Can you imagine me getting a word in edgewise?"

When I finished telling Buzzie about this, he calmed down and then he asked if the guy told us that he was conducting an interview.

When I said "No, we were just having a conversation, although it was mostly one way. . . with Carl doing the talking."

Buzzie got mad again and this time it was at the reporter.

He said "OK. I believe you, but we gotta do something about that reporter. He shouldn't be quoting people when it's not an interview situation."

You need to write a letter to him saying that his conduct was unprofessional . . "

I interrupted him and said "You bet I'll write him a letter ..."

Buzzie interrupted me and said "No, no, no! I'll write the letter and you'll sign it."

That was the end of the situation. He started out being very mad at me and when he finished, he told me to forget about reporting to the St. Paul clubhouse. So I went to the ballpark that night because we had another night game.

Like I said . . he had a temper but would listen to reason.

Cincinnati Offers 50 Grand for My Contract
In 1957 I had a pretty good season with the LA Angels in the Pacific Coast League. I had 11 wins and five losses, despite the fact that we had a sixth place club. On top of that, I was out for a total of about six weeks, once with a cracked rib and then a knee injury.

It must've been a pretty good year because one day, after the season, I picked up the newspapers and saw that the Cincinnati Reds had offered $50,000 to the Dodgers for my contract.

I was very excited at the opportunity to get out of the Dodgers organization. I realized very early in my career that I had made a mistake signing with the Dodgers. They had great pitching, so there were very few opportunities.

I remember reading an article in Sport Magazine near the end of my first year of professional baseball. The article featured Eddie Matthews who was playing for the Boston Braves at 20 years old.

In the article he was quoted as saying that although he had better offers from other teams, he picked the Braves because they hadn't had a solid third baseman for several years, and he knew that if he performed well, he would get a chance to make the team quickly.

My first thought was "Oh no! I should have signed with the Red Sox."

That's because in that era, their pitching was usually very poor.

Proof of that is that the next February, when before spring training started in 1954, I read in the papers that Truman Clevenger was going to be given an opportunity to pitch for the Boston Red Sox in spring training. Clevenger was in the same Class C California League that I was in the previous year. He made the team and had a fine career, but the point is, he was given the opportunity.

So when I saw the Reds wanted to buy my contract for $50,000, I called Buzzie and said "Sell! Sell! It's a profit of $15 grand."

He told me that he turned down the offer because they had plans for me that year; maybe even in the rotation. So I'd be given lots of opportunities in Spring Training.

I pitched a total of four innings against other major league clubs in Spring Training and was sent to AAA Spokane.

Sending Chuck Essegian to the Majors
It was late July, 1959. I was in AA Texas League having a pretty good year. By reading the papers I knew that the Dodgers were in a pennant race, and I also noticed that one of their pitchers, Gene Snyder, hadn't pitched in about four or five weeks. I was sure this was because Alston had lost confidence in him. I saw an opportunity and decided to call Buzzie.

I got Buzzie on the phone and the first thing I said was "You're in a pennant race. I'm getting my curveball over. I can help you."

He said "Who the #$*&@ is running this organization? Bavasi or Mauriello?"

I said "Calm down Buzzie. You know you're running the organization, but you're always open to suggestions. And as I said, you're in a pennant race. I'm getting my curve ball over and I can help."

He said "Well we have a full roster. There's no room for you."

I said "You have a pitcher who isn't helping"

And as quick as possible he said "Well he ain't hurting us either."

I came back as quickly as I could and said "That's because he's not pitching. Alston won't use him. If he's not pitching, he's not helping."

There was a long pause and then Buzzie said "You know, you might have something there Ralph. Let me think about this and I'll call you tomorrow."

When he called the next day I was excited because the first thing he said after hello was "You're right Ralph. Snyder isn't helping us, so I decided to option him to Spokane."

I quickly said "Great when and where do you want me"

He said "Well, I figured we were getting along fine without him. We *are* leading the league. So I decided another hitter would help and I called up Chuck Essegian from Spokane."

So that is how I sent Chuck Essegian to the big leagues.

In retrospect, and looking at it without any bias, it's clear that Buzzie made the right decision. They won the pennant without that extra pitcher, and Essegian hit two home runs during the World Series to help the Dodgers beat the Chicago White Sox.

That's what makes a great General Manager . . the right decisions.

Ron Perranoski and $5,000 loan request

Ron Perranoski and I were teammates in Montreal in 1960 and we really hit it off. We became good friends so even though I retired from baseball after the 1960 season, we still kept in touch. When he joined the Dodgers in 1961, he'd leave us tickets for the Dodgers games, we'd play a round of golf once in a while, have dinner with the wives and that sort of thing.

It was in the off-season after the 1961 season when Ron came to me with a problem. He and Sue (his wife) had found the house that they wanted in the San Fernando Valley, but they didn't have the $5,000 they needed for a down payment.

Ron knew that I had received a big bonus from the Dodgers and that I probably had some money in the bank. So he decided to ask me if I would loan him the money.

Most of my money was in the stock market, and at that time the market was down. I told Ron that in order to loan him the money, I would have to sell some stock and take a loss. So I couldn't loan him the money.

I told him "Why don't you see Buzzie and ask him for a loan. I'm sure he'll consider you a good risk."

He took my advice and went to Buzzie. Now the rest of this is hearsay because I wasn't there, but Ron told me all about his meeting with Buzzie.

Ron said that when he went into Buzzie's office and asked him for the loan, Buzzie leaned back in his chair and said "Ron you had a pretty good year last season, didn't you?"

Ron had a great year out of the bullpen for the Dodgers in '61. He was in 53 games with a 7 win- 5 loss record and an ERA of 2.65.

Then Buzzie reached into one of the desk drawers and pulled out a blank contract, back dated it April 1, 1961 and wrote in a salary that was $5000 more than Ron had earned during the 1961 season. He signed it and passed it over to Ron and said "Here I need your signature."

After Ron signed it, Buzzie took the contract back, and said "Looks like I owe you $5,000."

He reached into his desk drawer, took out a check book and wrote out a check for $ 5,000 and handed it to Ron.

Ron thanked him, and as he was walking out the door, Buzzie said "You had a good year last I season. I expect you'll come back and ask for a raise. I'll see what I can do"

"Talk to Fresco"
My last official interface with Buzzie was in May of 1960. That was the year that I decided to skip spring training and take some classes at USC that were only offered during the spring semester.

When I started playing baseball I realized that even a successful career would be over by 35 or 36, so I had to prepare for a career after baseball. My plan was that I would play baseball in spring and summer, and go to school in the winter. I planned to major in Electrical Engineering.

52

When I got my bachelor's degree, I would check my baseball career. If I wasn't in the major leagues I would quit baseball and start a career as an electrical engineer.

One of the problems with that approach was that there were a number of classes that simply were not offered in the fall. In January 1960, I was 21 units short of my degree, and most of those units were in classes that I could only take in the spring. So I enrolled for the Spring semester.

As the semester was ending, I decided I should play ball the rest of the season, because I couldn't make that kind of money as a junior engineer. I stayed in shape by throwing batting practice to the USC varsity, and for the Dodgers when they were in town, so I was ready to report to a Triple A club for the rest of the season.

I called Buzzie to ask him where he wanted me report and he coldly said "When you decided to stay in school, we sold your contract to Montreal. Talk to Fresco! You're his responsibility now, not mine."

Like I said he had a temper.

So I called Fresco and he sent me to Montreal. I joined them in June and finished the season with a 7 win 5 loss record for a team that finished in the league cellar. It was a respectable way to end my baseball career.

After taking my final classes at USC in the fall, I started my engineering career in January, 1961.

There's more about Buzzie and "meal money" in Chapter 16.

Fresco Thompson - VP of Minor League Operations

In 1952, I was selected as a representative of the city of Los Angeles to play a high school All-Star game in New York City. It was the New York City All-City team against a National All-Star team of high school seniors from around the country.

During the one week of workouts before the game, I was selected as the starting pitcher and pitched the first two innings, striking out three and allowing one hit.

By the way, Tony Kubeck, Yankee shortstop, and Bobby Locke, Cleveland pitcher, were on our National team.

We worked out at the Polo Grounds for a week before the game. One day during workouts, I was introduced to Joe DiMaggio and a photographer suggested we pose for a picture. It was a great thrill.

After the game, I was invited to work out with the Yankees and the Dodgers. Although it was a thrill to have Hall of Famer Bill Dickey catch me during my Yankee workout, I was looking forward to my Dodgers workout.

Me warming up in Ebbets Field in 1952; Author's collection

After a couple of workouts at Ebbets Field, I was invited to the Dodgers home office on Montague Street in Brooklyn to negotiate a contract.

54

That's when I met Mr. O'Malley, but he never said a word during the negotiations. Fresco Thompson, the Vice President of Minor League Operations for the Dodgers, did all the talking.

The initial offer was a $25,000 bonus. When I told Mr. Thompson that I already had a better offer from the Red Sox, he increased the offer to $35,000.

Although I had an offer of $40,000 from the Red Sox, I wanted to be a Dodger. After all, I was born and raised in Brooklyn until I was 14.

I remember asking Fresco "Let me see if I can understand what this bonus means. What happens to the money if I walk out of here and get hit by a truck crossing the street?"

Fresco answered "The money goes to your parents."

I said "Okay. Where do I sign?"

Now that we had agreed on a bonus, the next issue to settle was a contract for my services for the 1953 season. (Since it was late August, it was too late to consider sending me anywhere to the minor leagues that year).

Fresco drew out a blank contract and said "We will send you to a Class C league . . . Santa Barbara with a salary of $175 a month. OK?"

I said "$175 a month? How can I live on that? I need more than that to live. I don't want to be taking money out of the bank just to eat."

Fresco turned and said to Mister O'Malley "How do you like that? This kid just stuck a gun in my ribs for $35,000 and now he wants a salary raise before he's even thrown a pitch."

Then he said "Okay. How about $300 a month and a Class A contract with Elmira New York.

I said "Sounds good! Where do I sign?"

By the way, if you're wondering where was my agent? In those days nobody had agents. The ball players negotiated their own contracts.

And if you're wondering why I had offers from different clubs, it was because it was years before the draft was started, so I was a free agent.

Driving My Car to Spring Training
In 1955, I had been asked to come to Spring Training early; at the same time as the major leaguers. (The minor league training always started a couple of weeks later.) Because of that, somebody in the front office made a mistake and sent me the same letter that they send to the big leaguers.

The letter said if I wanted to, I could, drive my car to spring training and get reimbursed for the trip. Since I had just bought a brand-new car, a 1955 Oldsmobile "Rocket 88", I couldn't resist the urge to try it out and drive it from California to Florida.

When I got to spring training I wanted to get reimbursed for the gas money. In order to do that, I had to talk to Fresco Thompson. Although I was invited to workout with the big club, I had a minor league contract, and because of that I was Fresco's responsibility.

So I submitted a form for reimbursement to Fresco, and after about a week or 10 days, I still had not gotten a check, so I approached Fresco and asked about the delay.

He said "You're a minor leaguer. You're not authorized to drive your car to spring training. So you're not entitled to be reimbursed. If you chose to drive your car, that's on your nickel."

When I told him that I had received a letter authorizing me to drive my car and be reimbursed for the expenses, he didn't believe me. I had to call my dad and have him mail the letter to me.

When I showed the letter to Fresco, he said "I'm not responsible for what they do in the big league office. Somebody made a mistake! You shouldn't have gotten this letter. I'm not giving you a dime."

By now I was fit to be tied and stormed away and I happened to run into my buddy Jim Gentile. He didn't have a big league contract either, but he had driven his car and gotten reimbursed.

When I told him about the problem I was having getting reimbursed from Fresco, he laughed and said "Don't deal with him. He'll nickel and dime you to death. Go to Buzzie. (Bavasi:Dodgers General Manager). That's how I got my money."

I went to Buzzie and told him the whole story. He laughed and said "How much are you trying to get from Fresco?"

When I told him, I think it was $98, he laughed some more and said "Okay I'll write you a check."

Later that night at dinner, he came to my table and gave me a check for $191. When I looked surprised he said "That's the airfare from LA to here and I think you're entitled to it."

Tom O'Conner - Victoria, Texas Owner

At the end of the 1957 season, two teams dropped out of the AA Texas league, Oklahoma City and Shreveport. So naturally the Texas league was looking for new cities.

I was told that a Texas millionaire, a Mr. Tom O'Conner, approached Fresco Thompson of the Dodgers with a proposal that went something like this "Will the Dodgers give me enough AA ballplayers for my franchise so that I'll only lose $100,000 next year?"

I guess Fresco said yes, because a short time later, a Texas League franchise was awarded to Victoria, Texas, the home of Mr. O'Conner.

His daughter was the reason for all of this. She had dated one of the ballplayers from the Victoria ball club during the 1957 season when it was a Class B ball club in the Texas State League.

Yes, Mr. O'Conner was the owner of the Class B Victoria club.

The ballplayer was Don Miles, who had a "cup of coffee" with the Dodgers in 1958 (22 at bats).

Since Miles was scheduled to move up the ladder from Class B to AA, Mr. O'Connor decided to get a AA franchise so his daughter could continue to date this very good looking ballplayer.

Tom turned out to be a wonderful owner. Not only did he have the ballplayers out to his ranch on several occasions for barbecue and beer, (he was a cattle rancher) he really supported his ball club.

In 1959, the Texas League played an interlocking schedule with the AA Mexican League. I guess it was to increase attendance. The Mexican League had six teams and we were scheduled to play each team six times; three in our park and three in theirs.

It was about the middle of the season. We had just come back from Mexico, where we played in Nuevo Laredo, Monterrey and Mexico City. Nine games in nine days.

We flew in from Mexico City and got to bed about 5 or 6 in the morning . . . and we had a game that night. So naturally, that night, during the ballgame, we were dragging . . . and we were losing. It wasn't a pretty sight.

I guess we were doing so badly that the fans got upset and started booing us. That's when Mr. O'Connor went into action. He grabbed the microphone from the public address announcer and scolded the fans.

He said (please imagine a Texas accent):

"See here every body! Our boys are doing the best they can. They may be losing tonight, but they're leading the league. So they're doing just fine. Now if don't like the way our boys are playing, I'll refund your money for tonight, and then I'll close the ballpark for the rest of the season, and have the boys just play for me and my daughter."

Of course, I'm paraphrasing what he said, but that's what I call support from an owner.

Chapter 7 Some Characters I Knew

Steve Bilko

When I say "Bilko", you probably think of the 1996 movie, Sgt. Bilko, with comedian Steve Martin or maybe the popular TV series with funnyman Phil Silvers. Actually, they borrowed the name from Steve Bilko, a legend in the Pacific Coast League.

Bilko was the talk of the town. He was as big as the biggest Hollywood celebrity from 1955-57 when he hit 148 home runs to become the "King Kong of the PCL," a minor league with an open classification and just a notch below the majors in quality.

Steve hit thirty-eight homers in 1955, fifty-five in 1956 and fifty-six in 1957 when we were teammates. The league record was sixty.

For some reason, Bilko never came close to those numbers in the majors. He had seventy-six homers in parts of ten seasons. I was mystified with his inability to hit big-league pitching.

The first thing that comes to mind when I think of Bilko is how even tempered he was. I saw him get angry only once, and that was in batting practice.

I had been injured and was working my way back into shape before going on the active list. Since I was working on recovering, I was throwing all my pitches (fastball, curve etc.).

As is the custom for batting practice, whenever I threw something other than a fastball I would tell the hitter. When pitching to Steve, I forgot to tell him that I was throwing a changeup. He swung, missed badly and screamed at me because I didn't tell him what was coming. Again, this was the only time I ever saw him lose his temper.

The next thing I think of is that despite being a home run hitter, he was a very humble guy and a team player -- unusual for a big slugger. Near the end of the season I was pitching against the San Francisco Seals.

The game was scoreless when Steve came to bat in the third inning with everyone pulling for him to hit another homer and set a team mark of fifty-seven.

Instead of swinging for the fences, he slapped a grounder to the right side to score a runner from third base.

We were in sixth place, twenty-one games behind the Seals and yet Steve put the team ahead of his personal goals. The win was more important to him than a home run record. He was the ultimate team player.

As I said, a team man. Oh yes, his "sacrifice" wasn't wasted. We won the game.

Steve also watched out for rookies. I was a rookie when I played with him in '57. One day after a game in Portland, he asked if I wanted a great steak.

I said yes and went with him and Elvin Tappe, a catcher, to a "railroad car" diner somewhere in a poor section of town. There were no tables, only a counter with stools. Sawdust covered the floor. It didn't look promising until the steaks arrived. He was right. It was a great steak.

I was glad I didn't have to pitch to Steve because he was a terrific hitter. As a fielder, he had soft hands so he could dig out the bad throws and handle the ground balls that he could reach. Unfortunately, he didn't cover a lot of ground.

"Luscious" Luke Easter

Bilko was a big man, but not as big as "Luscious" Luke Easter. He was over 6'4" tall and weighed over 240 pounds. And he had the strength to go along with the size. He not only collected a number of minor league home run titles, but also hit a number of homers setting record distances.

In fact, he hit the first ball into the centerfield bleachers in New York's Polo grounds. If you're not familiar with the Polo grounds it was 483 feet to the centerfield bleachers.

Luke was a star at every level - negro league, winter league, majors, and the minors. The legends were about how far he hit his homers.

And he loved the legends about him too. When a fan told him that he had seen the longest homer Luke had ever hit, Luke said "If it came down it wasn't my longest".

I faced Luke Easter in the International League in 1960, several times I'm sure, but the only time I remember was when I "partially' faced him. What do I mean by "partially"? You'll see.

It was late in the '60 season. We were in Rochester and it was late in the game. I was pitching and we were ahead by a run or two. It was two out and they had a couple of men on and Luke came up as a pinch hitter representing the tying or winning run (I don't remember which).

Since Luke was a left handed hitter, I started him as I often did with left handed hitters; a slider up and in. He hammered it nine miles out of the park . . . but foul by ten or 15 feet.

I was on the mound rubbing up the new ball, facing left field, when I heard, or felt, somebody behind me. It was our manager, Clay Bryant. He told me he wanted to bring in a left hander, Wade Browning. I argued that I got what I planned for . . . a "loud strike" and was ready to work on Luke.

He insisted, and oddly he was almost apologetic. He wanted the left hander and he did bring him. As I recall, Browning got the out, and we went on to win.

The next day during batting practice, Luke came up to me and said "Ralph, I've been playing this game man and boy for over 30 years and I ain't never seen a man taken out because of a foul ball".

I smiled and said "Well that makes two of us."

Luke was not only a legend because of his long homers, but apparently Luke was born in several different places on different dates. For most of his professional career, he said he was born in 1921, in St. Louis, MO. Near the end of his career, he announced that he really had been born in1914 . . . and in a different town, Jonestown, MS. In later years, he said that maybe he was born in 1911 . . . or maybe 1915.

Sadly Luke died a very tragic death. He was living in Cleveland in 1979 and was a Chief Union Steward for the Aircraft Workers Alliance. He was leaving a bank carrying $40,000 in union funds when he was stopped in the bank parking lot by two robbers. When he refused to turn over the money, he was shot in the chest with a shotgun blast and died.

Rocky Nelson

Earlier in this book I talked about how pitchers setup hitters, but Rocky Nelson taught me that smart hitters set up pitchers. I know you're saying who was Rocky Nelson?

Rocky was a first baseman in the Dodgers organization with the misfortune of playing at AAA Montreal when Gil Hodges, a perennial all-star, was playing first base for the Dodgers.

In 1953, '54 and '55 Rocky had three seasons where he hit over .300 with his best year in '55 when he hit .364. He also had 102 homers during those three years.

But he had no place to go because Gil Hodges was playing first base for the Dodgers. Finally in 1956, the St. Louis Cardinals picked up Rocky off the waiver list, and he had a chance to play in the big leagues.

Sadly, he didn't do that well. He spent portions of nine seasons in the big leagues with five different teams and had a total of 620 at bats. Ironically, his lifetime big-league batting average of .249 was the same as Bilko's.

It was a spring training game, and Rocky was my teammate and he was batting against a left-handed pitcher. Rocky was a left-handed hitter. He swung and missed at a curve ball and looked so bad striking out that I couldn't look him in the eye when he came back to the bench to sit down.

He probably sensed my discomfort because he looked at me and said "Hey, kid. I just set him up for later in the game."

He saw the surprised look on my face and said "I looked intentionally bad on that pitch, because there's nobody on base. And I know later on in the game, there's gonna be a couple of men on base, and he's gonna try and get me out with that same pitch. And I'm gonna hit a line drive somewhere. Watch."

Later in the game, that situation came up. Rocky got the pitch he was looking for, and hit a line drive to right-field for a double and two RBIs.

Frank Howard

I remember when Frank Howard reported to the Dodgers' spring training camp at Vero Beach, Florida, in 1958 with a lot of fanfare because he was a gigantic six-foot-seven and 255 pounds. He signed for a big bonus out of Ohio State University where he was an All-American in both basketball and baseball.

So naturally when he took batting practice I was very interested. I was standing in centerfield shagging fly balls (as pitchers are supposed to do in batting practice) when he came to the plate.

Connie Grob, a pitcher who spent one year in the big leagues (1956) with the Washington Senators, was pitching batting practice. As Connie threw one fastball after another, Frank hit shots all over, and out of Holman Stadium, where the Dodgers played spring training games against other big league teams.

Then Connie looked at Frank, and twisted his wrist to tell Frank that he was going to throw a curve ball. This is common courtesy. It's batting practice, not pitching practice.

Connie didn't have a great curveball. It was the kind that we called a "nickel" curve. With good control, a live fastball, and guts, you could pitch successfully. Connie had all that, but he didn't have much of a curve.

In spite of the fact that Frank knew a curve ball was coming, he swung and missed. And he swung and missed every time. I put that in my mental notebook knowing that sometime in the near future I'd be in an intra-squad game, and Frank would come to the plate.

And sure enough a couple of days later, I was on the mound when Frank came to bat. Holman Stadium was 340 feet down the lines, and 400 feet to center. So it was a big ballpark. Instead of a fence around the outfield, there was a bank of grass about five feet high with a forty-five degree incline. So the bank served as a fence.

The fiasco of Frank trying to hit Connie Grob's curveball, when he knew it was coming, was fresh in my mind. I was pretty confident he would have trouble hitting my curveball. I threw two curveballs and he swung and missed both.

That's when I decided to get smart. I thought I could sneak a fastball by him on the outside corner. I didn't sneak it by him. He hit a bullet into right-field that was hit so hard, it stuck in the bank that surrounded Holman Stadium.

I learned my lesson. From then on every time I faced Frank in spring training, I threw him three curveballs. He would swing and screw himself in the ground and then sit down. He just couldn't hit a curveball.

Later that year we were teammates at Victoria, Texas, in the Class AA Texas League. I was scheduled to start the next night so I was in the grandstand behind home plate studying the opposing hitters.

The opposing pitcher was Terry Fox, who went on to become a fine relief pitcher for the Detroit Tigers. Terry had a great curveball and he struck out Frank four times with one curveball after another.

In 1959, the Texas League had a lot of young hard throwers with poor curveballs, and that allowed Frank hit .371 with twenty-seven homers. He was promoted to the Dodgers in June, but only for a short period of time (23 plate appearances) before he was sent to Spokane in the Pacific Coast League.

It was probably done this way to placate the owner of the Victoria club because the Dodgers knew that the he wouldn't complain about losing his star to the big leagues.

Frank went on to hit 382 home runs in the majors, including three consecutive forty-plus homer seasons for the Washington Senators. They called him "The Washington Monument." Obviously he learned how to hit a curveball.

Another thing about Frank; he wouldn't listen to anybody but the manager. At least he wouldn't listen to me. I tried to coach him on a situation where he missed the cutoff man and eventually caused the tying run to score in the ninth inning of a game. We lost the game in the 10th inning.

With a man on first and one out, the opposing batter hit a shot down the right-field line that went into the corner against the fence; 330 feet from home plate. Frank charged into the corner, picked up the ball and fired it all the way home plate, ON A FLY. (He had a great arm) He was trying to get the guy who was on first when the ball was hit, and was now heading for home. Not only was the guy safe at home, but the batter instead of getting a double, wound up at third base; because Frank didn't throw to the cutoff man.

Since it was the ninth-inning we had to bring the infield in and the next guy hit a pop-up that landed on the grass about four feet past the infield grass behind the second baseman. With the infield in, the ball fell in for a bloop single and the guy on third brought in the tying run. It would have been an easy out for the second baseman, if he was in normal position, as he would have been if the runner was on second base.

The next guy struck out, so it was clear that missing the cutoff cost us a tie, and we lost the game in the 10th inning.

The next day, when I explained to Frank that because he failed to hit the cutoff man it cost us the ballgame, he snapped at me and said "Pete didn't say anything." Pete was our manager Pete Reiser.

I responded by telling him to ask Pete what he thought of the play. I don't know if Frank ever asked.

"Choo Choo" Coleman

Clarence "Choo Choo" Coleman, was a catcher for the Montreal Royals in the AAA International League in 1960.

Based on what I saw, he wasn't too bright.

I'll never forget the time Bill Kunkel was on the mound. He pitched in the big leagues from 1961 to 1963, compiling a 6-6 record, and then umpired in the majors from 1968 until he died from cancer in 1985.

I was on the bench, so I couldn't really tell what was going on, but I saw Kunkel shaking his head over and over. He finally called Choo-Choo out to the mound for a conference.

After the inning was over, Kunkel came in, threw his glove on the bench and said "I can't believe this".

I said "What are you talking about Bill?"

Bill said "Do you remember the time I kept shaking Choo-Choo off, and finally I called him out to the mound?"

"Well, Choo Choo came out and told me 'Mauriello and [Babe] Birrer always get this guy out with a slider.' When I told Choo Choo that I didn't throw a slider he said 'Oh what would you like to throw'. Can you believe it's August and, he doesn't know what I throw?"

And that's not all. When Choo-Choo wasn't playing and one of our pitchers was on the mound, our manager, Clay Bryant, would walk by where he was sitting and say, "Choo Choo, quick! Tell me who's pitching?"

Sometimes Choo Choo didn't know. Bryant did that a lot. I don't know whether he was having fun with Choo-Choo, or if he was trying to keep his head in the game.

There's a side effect when you have a catcher that isn't too sharp. When you're thinking how you want to pitch to a hitter, and you've decided in your head that the curveball is the right pitch to throw, and he puts down two fingers for a curve, you start second-guessing yourself.

While Choo-Choo couldn't handle pitchers, he was a pretty good hitter at the AAA level. He had a decent arm, and he could run extremely well for a catcher. So he was drafted by the Phillies in 1961.

The next year he was picked up by the expansion New York Mets and he played parts of three seasons for them. Mets manager Casey Stengel once complimented Choo-Choo's speed by saying that he'd never seen a catcher so fast at retrieving passed balls.

Bobby Locke

Bobby Locke had a nine-year career in the big leagues, starting with Cleveland and ending with the Los Angeles Angels, with a couple of other stops in between.

Bobby Locke;
Courtesy of the
Cleveland Indians

I met Bobby Locke in 1952 when we were part of a high school National All-Star team that was made up of outstanding high school players from all over of the country. We were chosen to play against a New York City high school All-Star team in the Polo Grounds, home of the New York Giants before they moved west.

71

Bobby was from the hills of Pennsylvania, somewhere near Pittsburgh, and with the wisdom of coming out of the hills, he latched on to me because I lived in New York City until I was fourteen years old and knew my way around.

One of the first things he did was to come up to me in the lobby of the hotel, where we were staying, and say "Hey Ralph I need some tobacco. Where can I get some tobacco?"

I thought he wanted cigarettes, so I took him over to the cigar stand in the lobby.

"I want some tobacco" Bobby said to the guy behind the counter.

He said "What would you like? I've got Chesterfield, Lucky Strike . . ."

Bobby interrupted him and said "No! No! I want tobacco! You know, Red Man or something like that."

"Oh you want chewing tobacco," the guy said. "We don't have any, but there's a tobacco and pipe store around the corner and maybe they have some."

So we went around the corner and Bobby bought his tobacco. I knew about chewing tobacco, but I never knew anyone who chewed.

I never smoked cigarettes. In fact, I never even tried one. But I did smoke a pipe for a while when I got into engineering. After all, engineers want to look thoughtful and studious and smoking a pipe is supposed to have that effect. I only smoked a pipe for a couple years and then gave it up.

On another occasion, Bobby came with me to see a Broadway show. The organizers of the all-star game had arranged a number of activities for the players, and one of them was the Broadway show "The King and I" by Rodgers and Hammerstein.

The show is based on the book *Anna and the King of Siam*. The opening scene has Anna and her son on the ship that is coming into the port of Bangkok, the capital of Siam.

The boy looks out over the audience and says, "Mother, mother! I see men in boats coming towards us, and they look like they're naked."

We had great seats . . . .fourth or fifth row center.

Bobby stood up, turned around, looked at the back of the theater and said, "That kid's crazy. There's no boats back there. I'm getting outta here".

And he walked out.

Kenesaw "Kenny" Hemphill

Kenesaw "Kenny" Hemphill was from the hills of Arkansas and a self-professed hillbilly. We were teammates with the Mobile Bears of the AA Southern Association in 1955.

His biggest problem was he would disappear for two or three days at a time. When that happened, everybody knew that he was off on a drunken binge. He was always welcomed when he came back, because he was a pretty good pitcher.

At one point late in the season, Kenny disappeared for about a week. Since this was longer than usual, we all began to worry. But it turned out he wasn't on one of his binges.

He was bright eyed and bushy tailed when he finally showed up in the clubhouse one night before a game. "I betcha all you guys thought I was off drinkin' agin," he said. "But I wasn't! I went home to git married."

We all congratulated him. Then a couple of the married guys said they were taking their wives out after the game, and invited Kenny to bring his wife along so they could celebrate. Kenny told them his wife wasn't with him.

"She's at home 'cause she's gotta go to school," he said.

Almost all of us at the same time said, "School? How old is she?"

Kenny said "Thirteen".

That's right. In the hills of Arkansas, in 1955, getting married at thirteen was normal.

And I think that culture was best explained by Kenny when he told us this joke.

It seems this young hillbilly couple got married and of course there was a big celebration. When it was over, the couple went down to the cabin in the holler where all the young couples went to celebrate their honeymoon.

The next morning, the father of the groom is coming out the front door and adjusting the straps on his overalls when he looks down and sees Junior settin' on the porch.

The father says "Son whacha doing here? Yer supposta be down in the holler celebratin' yer honeymoon "

The son says "Pa, I had to come back. . . . She was a virgin."

74

Pa waits a second and says, "Ya done right son. If she weren't good enough for her own kinfolk, she ain't good enough for you."

This was a hillbilly telling a joke about his culture. Obviously Kenny didn't think twice about it. But to the rest of us, it was very unusual and strange.

Charlie "The Brow" DiGiovanni

Charlie DiGiovanni was the Dodger club house man for many years. He was running the clubhouse when I joined the team in 1958. He was a very happy and joyful man.

Charlie was responsible for making sure we had clean sweatshirts, jockstraps, socks and things like that. He also prepared meals for us between games of a doubleheader, and always had a lighter spread after every game so we could have a bite to eat or something to drink. Yes, he charged us for everything, laundry, food, drinks etc.

Charlie used to tout the purity of his food offerings by yelling out "Our food is untouched by human hands. We have apes in the kitchen"

Another of Charlie's responsibilities seemed to be that he had to give everybody a nick name. When I joined the Dodgers, the first thing Charlie said to me was "Mauriello! There was a heavyweight fighter by the name of Tami Mauriello. He fought Joe Lewis for the heavyweight title. Are you related?"

When I told him that I wasn't related, he said "That's okay, your nickname is still going to be Tami." and he wrote on a little card "Ralph Tami Mauriello" and put it over my locker.

I've always been glad that Charlie did that, because it allowed me to name my first daughter after me. Her name is Tami.

Another of Charlie's talents was that he seemed to know where all the deals were for the ball players. In every town there was a great fan who would give special prices to the ballplayers.

If you were looking for a suit, Charlie would tell you to wait for a certain town because there was a tailor there who really took care of the ballplayers. No matter what you were looking for, Charlie knew somebody, somewhere.

When I mentioned that I had proposed to my wife and was in the market for a ring, Charlie was quick to tell me that there was a jeweler in Cincinnati that always took care of the ballplayers. So when we got to Cincinnati, Charlie took me to the jeweler where I bought an engagement ring.

Charlie was an entrepreneur and always looking for a way to make a buck. One way was to book bets.

During one spring training camp, Charlie arranged for a foot race between Tommy Davis, Willie Davis and Maury Wills.

Yeah! That Maury Wills, the guy who stole 104 bases in a season. Everyone agreed these were the three fastest guys in camp.

It was setup as a 60 yard dash and of course, Charlie was booking bets. He was giving odds on each of the runners.

A lot of money was put down, and the betting favorite was Maury Wills, and the guy with the least money bet on him was Tommy Davis.

Me, Maury Wills and Tommy Davis at the 2008 Reunion; Author's Collection

They lined up, somebody yelled go, and off they went. At the 30 yard mark, Maury Wills was first, with Willie Davis a very close second, and Tommy Davis a full step behind in third.

As they went into the final 30 yards, Tommy Davis just sucked those guys up in his exhaust. He ran right by both of them and won the race going away.

We were all amazed and of course Charlie was very happy because he had booked a lot of bets on Maury Wills and Willie Davis, so he had a nice payday.

Sign the Baseballs

I don't know what it was like in other clubhouses, but in the Dodger clubhouse, there was always a dozen balls in a box that needed to be signed by all the ballplayers so they could be sold at the concession stand and help the club make a little extra money.

Charlie also had the responsibility to deliver six dozen autographed baseballs each week to the front office.

This gave Charlie another way to make money. Every day when we came into the clubhouse, there was Charlie yelling "Sign the baseballs. Sign the baseballs"

Most of us did sign the balls, but couple of the guys paid Charlie to forge their signature on the balls. I watched him sign a couple of balls, and he wrote the forged name just as easily as you and I would write our own name.

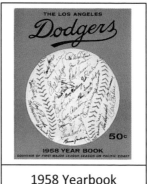

1958 Yearbook
Author's Collection

I also watched him sign the names of several very famous ballplayers, and I couldn't tell the difference between the real signature and Charlie's forged version.

In fact, years later, Duke Snider was quoted as saying "He could sign my name better than me."

And he wasn't limited to just a few of the big names. There are web sites on the Internet that claim that all the autographs on the 1958 Dodger Yearbook were signed by one man, Charlie DiGiovanni.

Like I said he was an entrepreneur.

Chapter 8 "Diamond" Jim Gentile

Why He Was Called "Diamond Jim"

While we're on the subject of characters, I must tell you about "Diamond" Jim Gentile." He wasn't called "Diamond Jim" because he wore a big diamond ring, but because of Roy Campanella and Charlie DiGiovanni, the Dodger Club house man.

It all started in Japan. Gentile went on a tour of Japan with the Brooklyn Dodgers, in the winter of 1956.

In 1956, he hit 40 home runs in double 'A' ball in Fort Worth. It was really tough for lefties to hit homers in that league. It was a combination of ballpark dimensions and the prevailing winds. So it caught the eye of the Dodgers.

He was invited to tour in Japan with the rest of the Dodgers team after the season ended and he caught fire. He hit .460 in 19 games and led the Dodgers in just about every offensive category during that trip.

While they were on the tour, a reporter asked Roy Campanella "What do you think of this Italian kid? "Campy said, "I think he's a diamond in the rough."

The next season when Gentile reported for spring training in Florida, the Brooklyn clubhouse manager - Charlie "The Brow" DiGiovanni - erected a sign over Gentile's locker that read "Welcome Home Diamond Jim." The nickname stuck.

Although he was stuck in the minors for seven years, Buzzie Bavasi, Dodger GM, was so impressed by the way Gentile swung the bat, that when a scout would call to tell Buzzie about some kid he was scouting, Buzzie would ask "Does he swing the bat like Gentile?"

Jim swung so hard that he actually hit his rear end with the bat on his follow through. He hit his rear end so hard and so often that he wore a pad on his left hip to absorb the blow.

"Diamond" Jim Gentile was a "victim" of Gil Hodges playing first base for the Dodgers during the 50s. Although he hit 208 homers in the minor leagues, the Dodgers had Hodges, so he

Jim Gentile taking the swing that Bavasi liked so much;
Jim Gentile collection

had no place to go. This was before free agency. Something called the "Reserve Clause" locked up all ballplayers to the team they originally signed with.

When he was finally traded to the Baltimore Orioles Jim had a fine major league career. He played nine years, and hit .260, had 179 homers and was an All-Star three times.

He had five grand slams in 1961, an American League single season record that stood until Don Mattingly belted six in 1987. Two of Jim's five slams were hit in the same game.

An RBI Title - 49 Years Later

Jim is unique because he was awarded the 1961 RBI title in 2010, 49 years later.

In 1961, Jim had a great year. He hit .302, with 46 homers and 141 RBIs. He finished third in the MVP voting behind Maris and Mantle. Yeah, that was the year Maris hit 61, and he and Mantle were dueling each other all year.

Originally, Gentile's 141 RBIs in 1961 was second to Roger Maris' 142 RBIs. The Society for American Baseball Research found out that Maris was credited, by mistake, with an RBI in a game on July 5, 1961. So Gentile and Maris both had 141 RBIs in 1961.

Jim Gentile getting his $5,000 forty-nine years later; Jim Gentile collection

In a phone interview I had with Gentile he said "After the season, when I was negotiating my 1962 contract with Baltimore general manager, Lee MacPhail, we argued over the contract. Finally he agreed on doubling my salary to $30,000."

Jim went on to say "I remember at the time I signed the contract, MacPhail said that if I had led the league in RBIs, it would have been worth $5,000 more."

Well in 2010, Jim got his five grand from Baltimore, after all. The former Orioles great was honored in a special ceremony before the August 5 game against the White Sox at Camden Yards. Orioles president Andy MacPhail, Lee McPhail's son, presented him with a check for $5,000.

What a Temper

Jim was a fun loving easy going guy . . . until he got on a baseball field. Then he expected perfection from himself and had a horrible temper when things didn't go right.

Locker in Mobile

One month after the start of the 1954 season, Jim was sent down from the AA Mobile Bears to the A Pueblo Dodgers. It wasn't because of poor performance, because in 34 games he had hit 8 homers and was tied for the league lead.

The reason was . . . it was "cut down date" in the big leagues.

In those days, the big league clubs would start the season with 28 players. Cut down date was 30 days into the season, when they had to get down to 25 guys.

So on cut down date, the Dodgers sent Rocky Nelson to Montreal (they had Gil Hodges), Montreal sent Norm Larker to Mobile (they wanted Rocky because he hit over .300 the year before) and Mobile sent Jim to Pueblo (Larker had a fine year for Mobile in '53).

Being sent down was always frustrating, but what really set off Jim's temper was the way he found out that he was being shipped out.

He had just finished infield practice before one of the games and he came into change his sweat shirt. He looked at his locker and his name had been removed and replaced with "Larker".

Jim asked the clubhouse man what was going on and the guy said " We're getting Norm Larker back. You're getting sent to Pueblo."

Normally, when a guy got shipped out (and I was shipped out a couple times myself, so I can speak from experience), the manager calls you in to his office and gives you a song and dance on how you're not cutting the mustard. But in this case of course Jim was doing real well, and what was more upsetting, was finding out from the clubhouse man.

Jim grabbed a bat and started attacking his locker. . . oops, now it was Larker's locker. When Jim finished attacking the locker, there was nothing left of the locker except the one hook in the back of the locker which was attached to the wall.

A fine display of temper, and believe it or not, he was not fined. Maybe the manager thought Jim was justified because of the way he found out.

Water Cooler in Phoenix
In 1958, Jim was playing for the AAA Spokane Indians when . . . Well, Let him tell the story.

> "*I struck out the first time up and everybody was hitting home runs and they were all talking about how well the ball flies in Phoenix. When I came up the second time and struck out, I got pissed. I was walking in the dugout and I saw the water cooler, and I hit it. It was like a bomb*

going off. Glass and water went everywhere. I wound up with 12 stitches in my ring finger. I was out for a week. The night I came back, I hit two homers. On the second one, I broke it open again and needed three stitches. The next night, I got a small sponge and taped it to my finger and got through it."

Breaking a Bat in Mobile

And there were times when Jim's temper was amusing.

It was late in the 1955 season and we were scrambling to make the playoffs. So every game, every at bat was critical. "We" were The Mobile Bears of the AA Southern Association,

We were in a tight ballgame in the late innings and we were at bat. We had a couple of men on and we were losing . . . I don't remember by how much.

Jim hit cleanup for us and was the next scheduled hitter. When the opposing manager brought in the left-handed pitcher to pitch to Jim (Jim was a left-handed hitter) our manager Clay Bryant did something very unusual.

I need to give a little background here. Earlier in the game, Jim had gotten our manager really pissed off. I don't remember what it was, but our manager was really upset. So upset, that with the game on the line, and our best hitter coming up, he sent up a pinch hitter for Jim. A guy named Ralph Rowe who was a 5 feet 7 inches, LEFT-handed hitter.

Jim was in the batter's box when the pinch hitter was announced. He stormed off the field, threw his bat in the dugout and kept walking on his way to the clubhouse.

I knew this was going to be one of Jim's famous tantrums, and since I wasn't pitching, I decided to go watch.

Let me set the scene for you.

Our clubhouse was a shack about 30 feet square with a big metal pole, 4" in diameter, holding up the roof. When I walked in, I saw Jim hitting that pole with another of his bats over and over. He was screaming that he was having a lousy year.

By the way at the time, Jim was leading the league in home runs and RBIs and hitting close to .300. So he was having a great year.

I remember jumping up on one of the trunks we used for shipping gear and having my legs dangle down. I said something like "Calm Down! Relax! You're gonna hurt yourself hitting that pole."

Jim screamed back at me "It's easy for you to relax 'cause you're having a great year" (I was on my way to an 18-8 season)

I said "And you're not?"

And with that he swung the bat so hard he broke it in two. No the roof didn't come down, but it was funny to see a guy who's leading the league in virtually everything, pissing and moaning saying he's having a bad year, because someone had pinch hit for him.

By the way, bats didn't break in two so easily in those days. I played eight years of pro ball and only remember a couple of times when a bat broke in two while a hitter was hitting. Now it happens two or three times a game. Now they use a very different kind of wood.

We Were Stopped, Not Arrested

Early one morning (say 6 AM) after a night of carousing with a couple of Houston's ladies, Jim and I found ourselves standing on the street corner of a residential district, a few miles from our hotel in downtown Houston. That's because neither one of us had enough sense to use a phone in the girl's apartment to call a cab before we left them.

While we were standing there trying to figure out what to do, some guy came by and I stuck out my thumb. He stopped and I told him we were staying at a hotel downtown and asked for a ride. He said he was going in that direction, but not near our hotel, but he'd take us as far as he could.

We hopped in and while we were going along, I saw a cab coming from the other direction. I waved it down, and we got out. Our ride drove off and we found out that the cabbie couldn't take us because he was on another call.

But he said "Wait here and I'll have 'em send out a cab for you"

"Here" turned out be a warehouse district. (This became important)

So now we were standing in this warehouse district waiting for a cab. After a couple minutes, a cab showed up, we got in and headed toward town. I was in the right rear seat and the right front window was open. After a minute or so, I leaned forward to roll up the window, so my pitching arm wouldn't get cold.

Right after I rolled up the window, we were pulled over by a police car. Jim and I sat in the back seat of the cab, while the driver got out to answer a couple of questions. While the cop was talking to the cabbie, Jim got madder and madder. He said to me things like "This Is America! Why are we being stopped! What's going on? "

After the cop finished with the cabbie, he asked us to get out and Jim continued his tirade. I finally calmed Jim down enough to tell the cop that "We're Fort Worth Cats and we're in town to play the Houston Buffs"

He looked at us and said "What? Who?"

Somehow we had come across probably the only cop in town who wasn't a baseball fan. He started asking us questions, and the more questions he asked, the more upset Jim became.

Then he told us that we were being stopped because of our suspicious behavior. He wanted to know what we were doing in that warehouse district at six in the morning. Were we casing a couple of places for a "hit" sometime later? Now Jim really started complaining about being stopped for no reason. And now I got nervous, because I knew that if I didn't calm Jim down we were going to wind up in jail.

I calmed Jim down, and finally convinced the cop that we weren't bad guys, and we were allowed to get back in the cab, go to the hotel, and grab a nap before going to the park.

It turns out that the thing that aroused suspicion was a couple of guys wandering around in a warehouse district at six in the morning. So the cop stopped to see what was going on. When the cabbie picked us up he decided to follow us.

The interesting thing is while we were on our way back to the hotel the cabbie told us "You know the first thing the cop asked me when I got out of the car was ' When that guy leaned forward, did he stash a gun in the glove compartment'"?

I guess the thing that caused the cop to pull us over was when I rolled up the window. So all this happened because I was worried about my arm catching cold. We didn't stick our arm in a bucket of ice like they do now

An Unusual Fan

We didn't have just female admirers!

There was this time when we were standing outside the hotel, killing a little time before taking a cab to the ballpark. Jim said "It's getting kind of chilly. I think I'll go up to the room and get a sweater."

I said "Okay I'll wait for you here. When you come down we'll go to the Park"

I thought about it a minute and decided he was right. It was going to get cool that night, so I figured maybe I should go back to the room and get a sweater also.

As the elevator doors opened on our floor, I saw a small guy holding his jaw, and it looked like he was bleeding. It looked like he had been in a fight. He got in and I got out.

I went to our room and as I opened the door there was Jim nursing his left hand. I could tell that he was upset and he said to me "Did you see that little fart?"

I said "Oh! Yeah. That must be the guy I saw at the elevator. What did you do? Hit him?"

Jim said "You remember when we were downstairs and I told you that I was going back to room?"

I said "Yeah"

Jim said "Well I walk across the lobby and this little guy gets up and heads towards the elevator right behind me. I get in and push fourth floor. He does nothing, so I figure he's on the same floor."

"When I get out of the elevator and turn towards our room, this guy follows. And when I put the key in the door, this guy says 'Mind if I come in?' That's when I turned around and popped him."

We shrugged it off picked up our sweaters and went out to the ballpark for the game.

Jim gets a chapter because he was my roommate (whenever we were on the same team), my best friend in baseball, and the best man at my wedding.

Chapter 9 Differences - Then and Now

The Knockdown Pitch

One of the things that's different about today's game is when a pitcher throws a ball anywhere close to a hitter. It doesn't matter that they're wearing helmets like they're in a war zone, anything close, and they start screaming at the pitcher.

In fact I was hit once in the back of the head on a three and one count. As the saying goes I got even the next time I was on the mound. It wasn't that I was that mean, we were taught that the knockdown pitch was just one of our pitching tools.

I was taught to knock a hitter down . . . not hit him. What you were trying to do was to intimidate the hitter.

I was taught that the best way to do that, was to throw at his head. That's because the instinct of self-preservation is very strong when the ball is coming at your head, and you can move it much faster than any other part of the body. At least that's what they told me.

In fact the culture of the knockdown was so much a part of the game that hitters, especially the good ones, expected to get knocked down once in a while.

In 1956, when I was in Fort Worth, I went through a terrible slump. For about 5 or 6 games I was having trouble getting past the 5th inning.

I was pitching against San Antonio and one of their big hitters, Bob Caffery, (funny how you remember the guys who hit well against you) hit one out the first time he came up. By then, I had a reputation . . . if you hit a homer off of me, you were going down the next time up.

But when he came up the next time I didn't knock him down. That night, after the game, I was in the local watering hole, where all the ball players would congregate, and nobody would believe this now, but Bob Caffery came over to me and said "Ralph, are you OK?"

Honest he did!

I said "Yeah, I'm OK. "

He said "When you didn't knock me down when I came up the next time, I figured something was wrong."

I looked at him and said, "Bob, I'm going so bad that I don't think I have the right to knock anybody down. I knock people down when I know what I'm doing and getting people out. I don't think it's fair to do that when I can't get the job done."

The point of the story is that the culture was so ingrained, that a guy would come to me and ask if I was OK because I didn't knock him down. By the way, we didn't have batting helmets in those days, just the soft cap that they wear when they're on the field.

Because of that we were taught how to react to a high and inside pitch. That was to rotate the head so the back of the head would be hit, if you couldn't get out of the way fast enough. Guys seldom got hit in the face like you see occasionally now. I'm sure now that the hitters have helmets, that lesson of how to deal with an inside pitch isn't taught anymore.

They're Bigger, Stronger and Make a lot of Money

I get annoyed when I'm around some of my contemporaries, and they say that the ballplayers of today aren't as good as we were.

That's baloney. All the athletes in *every* sport are bigger, stronger and faster than before. The main reason they're bigger and stronger, is better nutrition.

There are a couple of more reasons why the guys of today are much better: first, the salaries.

The players of today don't need a job in the off season. They can work out and stay in shape. The big leaguers of my day all had jobs in the winter.

Clem Labine designed sport shirts for a sportswear company. Carl Furillo worked for Otis Elevator. Carl Erskine worked in a bank, which was a good decision, because he wound up as president of the bank.

You get the idea. They didn't have time to stay in shape.

That's why Spring Training was invented. Because, during my era and also long before my time, most big leaguers had to work in the winter. They were out of shape when spring came around.

There's another reason why bigger salaries help make the players of today better. The potential income draws people into the sport who might otherwise do something else for a living. More people competing; better competition.

When I played, you had to love the sport to play it because the money wasn't that good.

We Ate Steaks, Not Pasta, Before a Game

Another thing that's different between now and then is food.

I can still remember my first clubhouse meeting when our manager was giving us a lecture about getting our rest (yes we had a curfew) and eating properly. He told us to stay away from greasy spoon restaurants and stay away from hamburgers and fries. And then out of a clear blue sky he turns and says to me "Mauriello, stay away from the pasta."

I did stay away from the pasta. I never had pasta on the day I was going to pitch. In fact, when I pitched, I usually ate a steak dinner about three or four hours before the game. We usually played night games that started at 8 PM, so I would usually eat about 4 PM. When we had a day game, I would have steak and eggs for breakfast. I was a fanatic.

I'll never forget how surprised I was when I heard Orel Hershiser being interviewed after a game and hearing him talk about having a big plate of pasta about three hours before he pitched because it gave a quick energy. We didn't know about that stuff when I played.

Hazing

You read and hear about how the rookies are forced to do stupid things like going to the airport in a dress or some other bizarre thing. When I played there was no hazing. In fact, I was welcomed and "looked after" by the veterans.

Don Drysdale always asked if I wanted to join him for a bite after the game. Carl Erskine was always offering advice.

I have a theory. Don't know if it's true, but I think it's because virtually all the American players have been to college and probably were in a fraternity, where hazing was part of the initiation. Even if they weren't in a fraternity, they probably were "hazed" by the veterans when they were new to the team. So they continue to do it.

I know for a fact, this was the practice at USC, when I went to school there. No, I didn't play on the team, because I signed a contract before entering college, but I knew all the guys on the team and heard the "horror" stories of what happened to the new guys when the team went on a trip.

I think that when these guys made it to the bigs, they decided to continue the tradition of hazing.

Pitch Count

Pitchers are coddled today and I think it's all because of pitch count.

First and foremost, we were expected to go nine innings. Now, a starting pitcher is expected to go six, maybe seven innings. Now you hear about a guy having a "quality start" if he goes six innings and gives up three runs.

In my opinion, it's "acceptable", but not "quality", because three runs in six innings is an ERA of 4.5, which is "acceptable" but certainly not "quality"

Also when I played, pitchers were on a four day rotation. You started every fourth day. Now it's a five day rotation.

Regarding pitch counts, all nonsense, in my opinion. When I played, nobody counted pitches. In fact, I remember that when I played, the last couple of innings were usually easier . . . for two reasons.

One, the excitement of winning usually pumped you up. Two, by the time you've been through the opposing line up successfully two or three times, you have a mental edge on the hitter. After all, a major part of the game is mental.

I don't understand why pitchers can only go about 100 pitches. It makes no sense; especially when you look at the readings of the radar gun after 100 pitches and see that the pitcher is still throwing as fast, or faster, than in the first inning.

I pitched a game one night where I gave up 12 walks, 5 hits and struck out 12 guys, and I might add, I struck out the side in the ninth. I had to. The bases were loaded.

How many pitches do you think I threw? Your guess is as good as mine. Nobody counted pitches in those days.

Yes, I finished the game and we won 2 to 1. The only run they scored was when somebody stole home on me in the eighth inning. After all it was my first year of pro ball. I guess I learned a lesson, because it was the only time it ever happened in my career.

And how many pitches do you think I threw in a 16 inning game while I was with Newport News. We lost that one 5 to 4 when our 2nd baseman made, not one, but three consecutive errors. Our 2nd baseman that night was Charlie Neal, who went on to have a fine big league career. So it can happen even to the best.

And despite the "coddling" of pitchers in today's environment, why do we seem to have twice the number of arm injuries when compared to the 50's and 60's?

I have a theory; too much weight lifting. It develops hard, tight muscles, most of which are of little value for pitching. Now you hear of pitchers who can't pitch because they've injured their bicep, a muscle that has very little to do with pitching.

We were specifically told to NOT lift weights. Nor should we do pushups, because it would tighten up the shoulders. We had a lot of "old wives tales" in our day, but never had the number of injuries that they do today.

In my day pitchers were told that they had to be able to get guys out with about a 90 percent level of effort. This was for two reasons:

1) When you got in a jam you needed a little something extra, something they hadn't seen before, to get out of a jam.
2) It would be very tough, if not impossible to pitch nine innings effectively at maximum effort.

No Water During the Game

When I tell stories about pitching in high humidity places like Houston or New Orleans, and how I sweat so much, people say things like "I bet you drank a lot of Gatorade or something like that on those days."

I tell them "We didn't have anything like Gatorade."

Then when I tell them that we were told to avoid drinking cold water while we were sweating because it would give us cramps, I usually see big eyes. They can't believe it.

Yes we were dehydrating and encouraged to do it. We could rinse out our mouth, but not swallow. Yeah things are really different now.

Batting Practice

Another thing that's different now is batting practice.

Some of you young readers probably wondered what I was talking about earlier in this book, when I talked about pitching curveballs and changeups and working on my pitches while I was throwing batting practice.

Now if you go to a game early to watch batting practice, you'll see some guy about 45 feet away from home plate lobbing the ball towards the hitter.

When we pitched batting practice we were told to put something on the fastballs so the hitters had something to work against. They wanted that so they were really practicing against something that they might see in the game.

Often after a batter saw a few fastballs in BP, he would ask for some curves or sliders so he could work on hitting pitches like that.

An example of that was during spring training with the Dodgers in 1958.

The Dodgers had a minor league outfielder, Felipe Monte-mayor, who was being looked at for possible promotion to the

Dodgers. But it turned out that Montemayor was having trouble hitting a curve ball.

One day in the clubhouse before our workout started, Alston said "Mauriello, you've got a good curve ball. Take Montemayor to the batting cages and throw him some curve balls so he can get better at hitting them."

We went to one of the batting cages and I threw countless curve balls to the guy and he kept swinging and missing. The best he could do was beat the ball into the ground. He didn't make the team.

When somebody is lobbing the ball from 45 feet away as they do now, it's pretty clear that the batter can't do anything in terms of working on his hitting other than perhaps loosening his muscles. It seems to me that the batting practice procedures today are of little value.

Infield Practice

The last thing that is different is infield practice. I used to always enjoy watching it . . . from the time I was in high school until I was retired and I'd go to a ballgame at Dodger Stadium. It was a choreographed drill just before the game and the purpose was to loosen up the guys so they were ready for the game.

They don't do it anymore. . . . and I miss it!!! Now when you go to a game and get there early enough, you see the guys jogging and stretching.

And finally, here are couple of minor ways that the game has changed. Infield chatter has disappeared from the sport. It's quiet out there and few players wear their pants in the old fashioned way. Those that do, look weird.

Oh well nothing stays the same!

Chapter 10 The Fans

God bless the baseball fans. Without them, we wouldn't have a chance to play a game we love . . . and get paid. You gotta love 'em but . . .

A Fan with a Straight Razor

When I was with Asheville in the Class B Tri-State League, we got into the playoffs and there was this one particular night in Greenville, South Carolina when emotions were running very high. Elsewhere in the book I talked about knocking down a hitter three times in a row under orders from the manager.

Later on in the same game, about the sixth inning, I was looking in to get my sign, when I heard the first base umpire call time. I turned around to see why the umpire was calling time, and then out of the corner of my eye I saw our right fielder running in toward the infield as fast as he could.

He was running because behind him was some guy in a pair of overalls, holding an open straight razor, chasing him.

I guess our right fielder and this fan were calling one another names and the fan jumped out of the right-field bleachers and started chasing him. It was a 4 foot high chain link fence so didn't take much for the fan to jump out and go after our right fielder.

A couple of the ball park security people tackled him and hauled him away. I guess he wound up in jail that night. No, I don't know if he was drunk or not.

We went on to win the ballgame, but when we left the field after the game, each one of us had a bat in our hands. We were afraid there might be some more crazy fans out there. I guess we were lucky because nobody challenged us.

Don't Like the Umpire's Call?

And then we have the case of the rabid fan that was so mad with a call by an umpire, that he dropped a chair on the umpire's head.

It was during my first year and we were on the road in York, Pennsylvania. We were ahead by two runs and I was called in to pitch with the bases loaded and nobody out in the bottom of the ninth.

I got a couple outs without anybody scoring and then the next guy hit a line drive to center field for a base hit. The guy on third scored easily, but the guy on second was called out at the plate trying to score. Our centerfielder made a great throw and the runner was out on a very close call.

I was backing up home plate, as a pitcher should, so I had a good look at the play. It really could have gone either way.

We got the call. That was the third out, the game was over and we had won by one run.

In order to leave the playing field in that ballpark, you had to walk down a narrow path between the grandstand and bleachers.

As the umpires were walking down that narrow path to their locker room, a fan in the bleachers dropped a folding chair on the head of the umpire who made the call. It was dropped from a pretty good height, because the umpire wound up in the hospital with a concussion.

A Fan Buys Dinner

Fortunately not all fans are sore losers. I remember in Memphis, I pitched a ballgame where a rabid fan sitting by our dugout was just constantly riding me. Of course it was nothing personal. He said things like "Spaghetti arm", "You're a bum", "What makes you think you can pitch" etc. All the usual things. Yeah, he had a very loud voice.

He screamed and yelled at me throughout the whole ballgame. When the game was over (by the way, we won), as I walked off the field after getting the last out, this guy started yelling "Mauriello I want to talk to you."

I ignored him at first, but the guy seemed like he wouldn't take no for an answer so I stopped to hear what he had to say.

I was really surprised when he said "I just have to tell you. You pitched a great game. But I had to do what I did . . . yelling at you throughout the ballgame, because I was trying to help my team win. But just to show you I'm a good sport I'd like to take you out to dinner."

My roommate, Jim Gentile, was standing next to me, (he stopped when I did) maybe just in case there was trouble. This guy looked at Jim and said "You're invited too."

We thought he was kidding us, but he said he was serious. So naturally we accepted . . . after all, a free meal is a free meal.

It was a good decision. He must have had a ton of money because he took us to a very fine restaurant in a brand-new Cadillac and we had a great dinner.

He Was Actually Proud

In 1960 I was with the AAA Montreal Royals. We were in Miami and just finished playing a day game and were headed to the clubhouse, when some fan called Ron Perranoski over to the stands. When Ron came to the clubhouse, he told me that the guy was regular at the Miami games and was an old friend of Ron's father.

Ron had been invited to dinner and a swim at this guy's house and said that he could bring along five or six guys. A couple of hours later, a half-dozen of us showed up at this guy's home.

It was truly elegant . . . just reeking with money. We had a nice dinner and after dinner sat around the pool talking. That's when this guy started telling us about how he made his fortune back in Jersey.

When he was a young man, he sold insurance for one of those insurance companies where the salesman had a route. He'd go to his clients and collect premiums every week.

Early in his career he was contacted by a representative of the local corrupt government and was asked to help in the re-election of one of the City Council members (or maybe an alderman) in some city in New Jersey.

He was told that since he was a respected member of his community, that if he did a soft sell on the candidate with his clients, he could probably swing his precinct in favor of the candidate. So he told them, he would do what he could but couldn't promise anything.

The first Friday after the election (by the way, the candidate he was supporting was elected) a motorcycle cop drove by his house and deposited a check in his mailbox. He had been named to a police commission and therefore was being paid by the city. He never attended a meeting, never was part of any commission but he collected a check every week for years.

Can you imagine this guy telling the son of a friend, and five perfect strangers, how he made his money. He was actually proud of his corruption.

Gambler in Memphis

Not all the people in the grandstand of ballgames are baseball fans.

I remember one time in Memphis, on an early trip, I looked up in the stands and saw 4 or 5 guys surrounding an empty seat. I could see two or three guys put their hands on the empty seat, and they had something in their hands. Then after a minute, one guy would pull his hand away and take what was on the empty seat.

It looked funny to me so I asked one of the veterans what was going on.

He said "Dummy! Those are the gamblers. They'll bet on anything. Whether the batter will get a hit or not! Heck they'll even bet on whether the next pitch is going to be a ball or strike, whether the next strike is going to be a swing and miss, or a foul ball. They're just here to gamble.

The next night, I pitched and after the ballgame I was walking to the clubhouse. In order to get to the clubhouse in Memphis you had to walk through an area where the fans were. Some guy came up to me, I'm pretty sure he was one of the gamblers that I saw the night before, and he said "You made a lot of money for me tonight. This is my way to say thanks" and he offered me a $20 bill.

Everybody in baseball knew that you must stay away from gamblers. So I thanked them and walked away. That was my only up close experience with a gambler in eight years.

How Fickle Can Fans Be?

In the 1955 AA Southern Association All Star game, Jim Lemon, hit four Home Runs. I was there. It was truly unbelievable. Lemon went on to a fine 10-year big league career at Wash-ington & Minnesota. He hit .262, with 164 home runs.

As luck would have it, several nights later, I was pitching against him in a regular Southern Association League game in Chattanooga, Tennessee. I was with the Mobile Bears, a Dodgers farm club, and he was with the Chattanooga Lookouts, a Washington farm club.

When he came to the plate in the bottom of the first, the bases were loaded and the Chattanooga fans gave him a standing ovation. When he struck out, most of the fans, but not all, rose and gave him another standing ovation.

When he came to the plate with two men on base in the third inning, the fans gave him another ovation, but remained seated. When he struck out, the fans cheered, but it wasn't quite as loud as when he came up to the plate

When he came to the plate in the fifth inning with the bases loaded, the fans cheered. When he struck out again, he was applauded, but it was a lot less than after his last time at bat.

When he came to the plate in the seventh inning with two men on base, there was a smattering of applause. When he struck out again, the stands were absolutely quiet.

Then a lone voice yelled out "You bum. Who ever told you that you could hit."

That's what I call fickle!!!

Snake in Monterrey Mexico

As I mentioned in an earlier chapter, in 1959 the Texas League played in an interlocking schedule with the Mexican League. One of our stops was Monterrey Mexico. The fans there were unique. When I looked up into the grandstand, I couldn't help but notice that there were no women in the grandstand; only men and boys.

I wondered why until a little later in the game I saw some strange happenings that made it clear to me why the ladies and girls stayed away from the ballpark.

At one point during the ballgame, when things were kind of quiet, some guy in a stands behind the first base dugout (we were in the third base dugout) stood up and started waving a snake over his head in a circular motion. I'd guess the snake was six to eight feet long.

As he was waving the snake, the people started running away from him. They were literally climbing on top of one another. The grandstand was really just a set of wooden bleachers; no chairs, so moving away was easy

One of the guys on our team, Phillipe Montemayor, was a native of Monterey, and he said "Oh, they do this sort of thing all the time at the ballpark. They have fun."

This guy waved the snake for a minute or so, and then he let it go. It sailed toward the grandstand behind home plate and then the people all started running in the other direction stepping on one another.

Then somebody discovered that the snake had its mouth sewn up (by the way, it was poisonous) so they all started laughing because it was a good joke.

They sure knew how to have a good time.

Later on in the game when Montemayor, the local boy, was coaching first base for us, somebody threw a small snake (maybe three or four feet) out on the field at the coach's box.

Naturally, Montemayor started running until he looked down and saw that the snake was harmless. Then he walked over, picked it up and threw it back in the stands.

Yes, Mexican fans are a lot different than American fans. In eight years of pro ball in the U.S. I never once saw somebody get up and throw a snake around the grandstand.

Autograph Requests

Believe it or not after all these years, and only three games in the big leagues, I still get requests for my autograph in the mail.

I get letters congratulating me on my fine major league career and would I be so kind as to sign the enclosed three by five cards. Sometimes I get a letter asking if I would sign a baseball.

Lately it's slowed down a bit. I used to get 25 or 30 requests a year. Now it's dwindled down to about 10 or 15 a year.

I used to get requests to sign five or six 3" x 5" cards and I would sign them all . . . until I discovered that these guys were selling my autograph on the Internet for $5 a copy. It seems that's all my autograph is worth. At least I assume it's actually selling for that price.

Because of that I now only sign personalized requests.

A few years ago, I got a package from a grammar school teacher in Brooklyn. The package had 19 photos of me and a request for 19 autographs. It seems her class decided to study the Brooklyn Dodgers as a project, and they decided to get the autograph of everybody who ever played for the Dodgers. If they wanted my autograph, they really wanted everybody.

Since I suspected that this was really a scheme to get a bunch of autographs so they could be sold on the Internet, I wrote back to the lady and told her that I will only sign personalized autographs, and I needed the names of each of the 19 kids.

She came back with the names of all 19 kids and I signed 19 photos and mailed them back to her.

I've actually gotten autograph requests from foreign countries; Canada, Germany, and Japan. The one from Canada had to do with the fact that I played for Montreal in 1959 and 60, and the one from Germany was an Army staff sergeant who was deployed in Germany and a very good baseball fan.

But the most amazing thing was to receive a letter from a young man in Japan who was an avid baseball fan and wanted my autograph. He had done research and he knew all about my career, as brief as it was, and wrote a very nice letter asking for an autograph.

Twice, and only twice, I got something in return. After signing a ball for a guy in Missouri, he sent me a coffee mug with the Missouri State Highway Patrol logo. Good quality logo because it's been through the wash for years, and still looks good.

The other item was not really a return for an autograph, because it was sent to me without a request for an autograph.

A truly GREAT fan of mine, Joe Hoppel of St. Louis, MO, sent me a copy of the scorecard being sold at Wrigley Field on September 19, 1958; the day of my first and only big league win. Absolutely amazing!

Of course I sent him an 8" x 10" autographed picture taken the day after my only win . . . along with my undying thanks

Chapter 11 Tom Lasorda

Tommy and I were teammates in 1957, with the Los Angeles Angels of the old Open Classification Pacific Coast League, and in 1959 and 1960 with the Montreal Royals of the AAA International League.

"Win One for the Baby"

When people find out that we were team-mates, they almost always ask "Is he really like that?"

What they're referring to is his constant cheerleader attitude. And I always tell them "Yes, he really is like that."

I've heard him say to me "They bawl me out because I'm a lousy strategist. I'm not a strategist, I'm a motivator, a motivator", and you know what, he always was.

Tommy and me on the bench in Montreal; Author's collection

Then I tell them that in the three seasons that we were teammates, I only saw him down one time. (I'll get to that later). The rest of the time he was always up and optimistic.

I always tell them about how Tommy behaved the night after our first daughter was born. Our oldest daughter was born in August 1960, while we were in Montreal.

As luck would have it, it was my turn in the rotation the night after she was born. Since we were at home, I went out to pitch the top of the first. When I came in after the first inning, Tommy was running up and down the bench telling all the guys "Come on let's go. Let's score some runs. We gotta win one for the baby."

Remember, he was one of the four starters in the rotation . . . not the coach, or the manager. I guess he was a good motivator, because we did win the ballgame 13-1, and I have the game ball in my trophy case.

San Francisco Seals Beat Down Tommy

Now I'll tell you about the only time I ever saw Tommy "down". We were playing for the Los Angeles Angels of the old Pacific Coast League in 1957.

We came in fifth or sixth that year. San Francisco, on the other hand, was loaded with guys who went back and forth between the Pacific Coast League and the Big Leagues and they won the league championship with a record of 101 - 67.

They won it by scoring so many runs that it didn't matter what the pitchers did. In fact, San Francisco had a guy with a five wins and no losses with an ERA of six or seven. He was shipped out to AA in the middle of May. Imagine being 5 and 0 and getting shipped out.

We were in San Francisco for a seven-game series, which was standard in the Coast League. We would play Tuesday night through Friday night, a Saturday afternoon game, and then a Sunday doubleheader.

During that series, they beat the crap out of our pitching staff. None of our starters finished (We were expected to finish in those days) and they simply wore out our bullpen.

We were sitting in the clubhouse after being hammered in the first game of the Sunday doubleheader . . . we'd lost five out of six, and every one of our starting pitchers had been nailed to the wall.

Clay Bryant, our manager held up the game ball and said "Who wants to pitch the second game?"

Tommy jumped up and said "Give me that ball. I'll go get those bastards."

Now you have to remember that he was in our rotation, and like me and the other two guys he had been hammered by the Seals earlier in the week. I confess that I don't remember whether he was knocked out of the box once, or twice, earlier in the week. But that didn't matter to Tommy. Always optimistic; he wanted the ball.

Tommy didn't get out of the first inning. It was one line drive after another. After Clay went out to the mound to take him out, Tommy came in with his head down and slammed his glove on the bench and said "What the #$*&@ ever made me think I could get those guys out."

That's the only time I ever heard anything negative come out of him, and I've known him for years!

The Coconut Grove

I like to sing and perform on stage. At this particular time I was in a musical called the Music Man, the one written by Meridith Willson.

One night at the rehearsal the director came up to me and said "I have a gig in LA. I have to get some entertainment together for a testimonial for Tommy Lasorda, the Dodgers manager, at the Coconut Grove. It's being given by the local Italian-American club. I need you to sing a couple of songs. It pays pretty good. Are you interested?"

The Coconut Grove was a first class night club at one time, but no longer exists.

Funny thing is he didn't know that I had played professional baseball, let alone was an ex-teammate of Tommy's.

I said "Sure it should be fun. Tommy and I were teammates for three years while I was playing baseball."

He said "Oh that's great! But what's really is important is I need you to sing this song for Lasorda. I wrote some words to an old country-western song called *My Woman, My Woman, My Wife* and I changed the lyric and the title to *My Father, My Father, My Dad* because Lasorda had such a close relationship with his father. I want you to learn the words and sing it for Lasorda."

A couple weeks later, I was on the stage of the Coconut Grove singing the song and Tommy was at a table right next to the stage.

When I looked down at Tommy, he looked up at me and mouthed the words "What the #$*&@ are you doing up there? He didn't say it, he just moved his lips. After I finished the song the director had written, I sang a song I called "Ode to Lasorda" sung to the tune of the old Sinatra hit, "My Way."

"Ode to Lasorda"

Sung to the tune of **"My Way"**

Lyrics by Ralph and Gina Mauriello;

And now the year is through, and so I face that rubber chicken,
I'll talk 'till I turn blue, better that, than my waist should thicken,
I'll tell about this year, about things that went astray,
And yes, I'm sure to say, we did it My Way.

Sore arms, more than a few, lot's more than I've time to mention,
And then, to make it worse, the press said we had dissention,
It's been a real tough year, In spite of guys like Garvey and Cey,
But still no matter what, we did it My Way.

Refrain
To call the plays, I truly feel,
And not the ones of the big wheels,
He said strike three, I thought ball four,
I charged the ump, and what is more,
He changed the call, and I stood tall,
He did it My Way.

Regrets, sure I've got some, but them again just wait 'till next year,
I'll do what I have to do and see it through without a fear,
I'll plan each stolen base, I'll figure each and every fine play,
And more, much more than this,
We'll do it My Way

Repeat Refrain

115

I should point out that it was during the off-season after a very poor year for the Dodgers. They had all kinds of injuries that season, I think it was 1982, and they came in second place to the Atlanta Braves in the Western Division.

After I finished singing, I came down off the stage and went to Tommy's table. Bill Russell, Ron Cey, Charlie Hough and Don Sutton were with him. He asked me to join them, and introduced me all around.

An interesting thing about Tommy's personality is that age comes first. When he introduced me to Don Sutton, who had an excellent curve ball, he said "Don you have a curveball just like Ralph's."

I had a very good curve ball and so did Sutton. Don said "You mean Ralph had a curveball just like mine."

Tom said "No, Ralph came first. Your curveball is like his."

He did that again one night during batting practice when we were behind the batting cage shooting the bull. While we were talking, Joe Garvey, Steve's dad, came over and started talking to us. Joe used to drive the bus during spring training at Vero Beach, Florida.

We spent a lot of time on the bus because the closest spring training camp was the Giants in Melbourne which was about a 30 or 40 minute drive. But when we went to Tampa which is on the West Coast of Florida it was a couple of hours. So we spent a lot of time with Joe Garvey.

We were swapping "remember when" stories, as you always do when get around guys you haven't seen for a while, when somebody came up to us, and Tommy introduced Joe as "Say hello to Joe Garvey. Steve is his son."

And the guy said "Oh you mean he's Steve's Garvey's dad".

Tommy said "No Steve is Joe's son. Joe came first!"

As I said, it's a peculiarity in Tom's personality.

Litton Management Club

Then there was the time I was the Entertainment Chairman for the Litton Management Club. (Litton was an aerospace firm that I worked for)

At that time Tommy was managing the Dodgers and I went to the games a lot. The tickets were free (Tommy or Ron Perranoski would always leave tickets) and it was fun going in the clubhouse and shooting the bull with the guys.

The "guys" I'm referring to were Tommy and all the coaches, who were guys I played with or against during my career. Tommy did introduce me to most of the ballplayers, but the real reason I went, was to talk to Tommy and the coaches.

One night when I was behind the batting cage shooting the bull with Tommy, it occurred to me that he would be a great speaker for our Litton management club. So I asked him if he would come speak at our club sometime during the off-season. He said "Sure. I'll have my agent contact you".

When the agent contacted me, I discovered Tommy's fee for a speaking engagement was $5,000. This was really a problem because all I had in the budget for a speaker was $1,200. I told the agent we couldn't afford Tommy.

On the next home stand I went to the ballpark and I was at the batting cage talking with Tommy and he said "Ralph I haven't heard from my agent about talking to your club."

When I told Tommy about my conversation with his agent, he exploded.

He said, "What? You say you have a budget of $1,200. What kind of a speaker can you get for that? A local TV weatherman?"

He hit it right on the head. One of the speakers that I had arranged for that year was "Dr. George", a TV weatherman. But he wasn't on a local channel. It was ABC network, Channel 7 for Los Angeles.

After all the ranting and raving, Tommy said "Ah what the hell. I'll do it for an old friend."

Now I was embarrassed. After speaking to Tommy's agent, I decided to ask Sparky Anderson if he would speak. And he agreed to the $1200 fee.

When I told Tommy that Sparky had agreed to the fee, he exploded again (yes he is emotional). After he calmed down, he agreed to speak for the $1200 fee.

Now I was embarrassed again. I had to tell him that all the monthly meetings for the year had been booked and I couldn't have him speak until next year.

He blew up one more time. Then he said "Okay. Call my agent. Set up the time and I'll be there." And indeed he was... and gave a great talk. He always does.

The Reagan Library

Recently, Tommy was the featured speaker at the Reagan Library here in Simi Valley, California.

When I heard he was going to speak, I contacted the organizer and told her "I was a teammate of Tommy's and I often sing the national anthem at Dodger Stadium. I can sing the national anthem just before Tommy speaks. And I know I can find an umpire who would be happy to come there and shout 'Play Ball' just before Tommy speaks."

She accepted my offer to sing the national anthem, but turned down the idea of an umpire.

I met Tommy at the elevator that took him to the floor where the auditorium was. He was being escorted by the lady who organized the event and Tommy

Tommy and me at Dodger Stadium, May 16, 2015; Author's collection

turned to her and said "Ralph and I used to sing a quartet together when we were in Montreal."

I was really surprised, because in all of the times that I had seen Tommy since I retired, he never once mentioned our singing together in a quartet.

We had Joe Altobelli, and Gordon Windhorn along with Tommy and me in a quartet. "Gordie" played the guitar and sang bass, Altobelli sang tenor, and Tommy and I both sang melody, because neither one of us knew a whole lot about music, at the time.

Gordie was a journeyman outfielder, who played with four clubs in three major league seasons. Altobelli, played with two teams in three major league seasons, but he went on to manage the Baltimore Orioles and led the team to their sixth American League pennant and their third (and most recent) World Series championship in 1983.

After I sang the national anthem, Tommy took the podium, and the first thing he said was "Ralph you're a whole lot better singer than you were a pitcher".

That stung a little bit, but I got even with him. After he finished his speech, he was given a bat to commemorate the occasion. I couldn't resist walking up to Tommy and saying "What are you gonna do with that bat? You were lousy hitter."

Maybe I was getting even for the time that I took my grandson to Dodger Stadium to see a Dodger game. We got there early, so we had a chance to go down on the field and talk to Tommy.

The first thing I did, of course, was introduce my grandson, Cameron, to Tommy. He looked at my grandson and said "Hello Cameron. Did your grandfather ever tell you how lousy a hitter he was?"

He may have been accurate, but it hurt.

I have another story about Tommy in the Havana chapter.

Chapter 12 Havana, Cuba

Dodgers to Havana

When I was with the Dodgers in spring training in 1959, we had a string of rain storms that washed out all of our workouts. We were sitting around in the lobby of the barracks at Dodgertown (it was an old Navy base) in Vero Beach, Florida, and playing cards waiting for the rain to stop, when we heard that we were going to Havana the next day.

We were told that Walter O'Malley, the Dodgers owner, decided that he had enough of the rain, and he was going to take his team to where the sun was shining; Havana Cuba. So he called Powell Crosley, who was the owner of the Cincinnati Reds and said "The sun is shining in Havana and I have an airplane. Let's fly both of our teams down there."

The next night we were in the big stadium in Havana getting ready to play the Cincinnati Reds an exhibition ballgame.

We finished our batting practice and were sitting in the dugout watching the Reds take infield practice, when one of the Cuban soldiers with his well-oiled machine gun slung over his shoulder, leaned over the dugout railing and said to Greg Mulleavy, "Pelota, pelota".

Greg was one of our coaches and his job among other things was to keep track of the ball bag, a big, thick leather bag with about two or three dozen baseballs in it, which we used for batting practice.

Greg made believe that he didn't understand what the guy was saying. He knew what a pelota meant. He was just hoping the guy would get discouraged and go away.

But the guy climbed over the railing into the dugout. He reached into the ball bag, pulled out a ball, showed it to Greg and said "Pelota".

Then he climbed back over the railing and walked away. A minute later another soldier walked up to the dugout railing and said to Greg "Pelota".

Greg knew that the guy he gave the ball to had showed it to his buddies. So he had no choice. He reached into the bag and gave the guy a ball.

Then there was a stream of guys, all in uniform, all carrying well-oiled machine guns. Each one came and said "Pelota".

Greg gave away one ball after another.

That's when Pee Wee Reese, our shortstop, and Captain said "For God sakes Greg, what are you doing? If you keep giving balls to those guys, we won't have any for batting practice."

And Greg said" Pee Wee, have you seen those guns? If they ask me for my jock, I'm gonna give it to 'em."

Tommy's Revenge in Havana

I was a teammate of Tommy Lasorda in 1959 and '60. We played for the Montreal Royals which was in the AAA International League. The International League was truly international. We had two teams from Canada, Toronto and Montreal, and we had the Havana Sugar Kings in Havana, Cuba. The other five teams in the league were in the United States in cities like Miami or Buffalo.

We went to Havana three times each season, and in 1959 and '60 it was after Castro had successfully taken over Cuba. In fact, I think it was January 1 of 1959 when Castro claimed control of Cuba.

During one of those trips, we were sitting in the lobby of the Hotel Nacionale when a bunch of guys in military uniforms carrying well-oiled machine guns came into the lobby shouting "Cuidado! Cuidado!"

Then they went on with a few more words in Spanish that I didn't understand. But Tommy understood Spanish very well and he yelled "Hey they're taking over the hotel".

Which of course was all part of Castro's plan; nationalize all the businesses.

Hotel Nacionale, Havana Cuba;
Hotel Nacionale website

By the way, if you've been going to baseball movies, you've seen pictures of buses and two-story motels in AAA ball. That's baloney.

When we were in Havana, Cuba, we stayed at the Hotel Nacionale. It was first-class then, and it's first-class now. And we weren't on buses; we flew from city to city.

Conditions in the minor leagues were nowhere near as bad as they portray in the movies; at least not at the AA and AAA level.

The result of the nationalization of the hotel was brought home to us that night after the game. A bunch of us were in the casino, and Tommy was playing the roulette wheel like you've never seen before.

It looked like a grade B-movie. He was putting chips on the table, playing four numbers at once, two numbers at once, and sometimes playing a single number. If there was a pattern, I couldn't figure it out. But he wound up winning $300. That was a lot of money in those days.

When he went to cash in his chips, we found out what it meant for Castro to take over the hotel, because they paid Tommy off in pesos. He started screaming saying "I put American dollars down, and I expect to be paid off in American dollars."

You have to remember that after Castro took over Cuba, the Cuban peso wasn't worth much in the United States . . . probably worth about 15 or 20 cents back in the US at that time.

No matter how long Tommy screamed and yelled, the guy behind the cage said "Sorry senor, but we must pay you in pesos."

So Tommy grumbled and took the pesos. But when we checked out of the hotel, two days later, Tommy got even.

When you travel with a professional baseball team, the team pays for the hotel room, and gives you meal money to pay for your meals. But the ballplayer is responsible for any incidentals that he charges while at the hotel. For example laundry, or maybe room service.

When I went to check out, Tommy was standing by the cage where we were supposed to pay for our incidentals. He said "Ralph, They're gonna demand dollars from you to pay your incidentals. Don't do it. Give that SOB pesos".

I said "I was planning to do that anyway. I have some pesos and they're not worth much in the states."

So I offered to pay my bill in pesos, and the guy behind the cage said, "Sorry senor, but you must pay in American dollars"

I said "I don't have any American dollars.

He said "Senor" . . . and that's as far as he got because I interrupted him.

I said "Whether I have dollars or not, this is Cuba and I want to pay in pesos."

"Sorry Senor. I cannot accept pesos"

Then Tommy said "Make the offer one more time I'm your witness".

I was glad he said that because if you don't pay your incidentals, the ball club will take it out of your check. I made the offer to pay in pesos one more time and the clerk refused it and requested American dollars again.

Tommy said "Okay Ralph. I've witnessed that you tried to pay, so you can go."

Tommy spent the whole morning by the cage telling every guy who came to pay his incidentals, to pay in pesos, so none of us paid our incidentals. By the way, Tommy was acting as our official travelling secretary.

I'm sure the hotel thought they would get their money in American dollars by billing the ball club. A few days later, when we were back in Montreal, we heard that the hotel had made a claim for payment of the ballplayers incidentals.

But the ball club refused payment saying that the ballplayers were responsible for their incidentals and it was witnessed that they tried to pay and the hotel had refused payment.

The Toronto Shortstop is Shot

Toronto and Montreal would travel as a pair of teams. For example, we would go to Miami and Havana. So when we were in Miami, Toronto was in Havana. Then we would switch cities.

Since I was with Montreal for parts of two seasons we made several trips to Havana. There is one trip that really stands out in my memory. It was 1960 and was in late July. We had been to Havana first, and then switched with Toronto. They went down to Havana, while we went to Miami.

We were in the Miami visitor's clubhouse on July 27, the day after Tommy made sure that we didn't give the hotel American dollars. I remember the date because in Cuba, July 26 is the day celebrated as the start of Fidel Castro's revolution.

We were getting ready to go out to batting practice when our manager, Clay Bryant, called a club house meeting.

Clay started out by saying "Guys I have something very serious to talk to you about. Last night the Toronto shortstop was shot while he was on the field".

We were all stunned.

Clay went on to say "It's only a flesh wound and he'll be okay, but we have something to think about."

"All the managers of the league have been contacted, and we've been asked to poll the players to see if they are willing to go back to Havana. What this means is, if we don't go back to play the games scheduled for our next trip to Havana, we'll forfeit those games."

At the time we were battling for a playoff spot, and if we forfeited those games we would have a very tough time making the playoffs.

Then Clay said "Every team in the league is being asked the same question, and I have no idea how the other teams are going to vote."

"I may be your manager and you have to do what I ask you to do on the field, but this is a personal issue and every man will have to decide for himself whether he wants to go back to Havana."

"Now I don't want to influence you in any way. All those who don't want to go back to Havana raise their hand".

As he said this, he raised his hand.

It was unanimous throughout the league. We all voted not to go back to Havana. The last two games of the three-game series between Havana and Toronto were canceled and Toronto flew back to Canada two days early.

Since that was the last game scheduled for the Havana home stand, the Havana team flew to somewhere in the US to play their next scheduled game. I don't remember where, but they were in the US when it was announced a couple of days later that the Havana franchise had been transferred to Jersey City, New Jersey.

So we never went back to Havana . . . with good reason. We were scared.

My Advice to President Kennedy

Before I leave the subject of Havana, I have to tell you about the dramatic changes that we saw in Havana during our trips there in '59 and '60.

In the summer of '59, everything about Havana seemed the same as it was before Castro took over in the hotel, restaurants, shops etc.

On the other hand, I'll never forget that when we drove down the main street toward the hotel coming from the airport, there were lots of peasants living in cardboard boxes on the sidewalks.

One year later there were no cardboard boxes on the sidewalks, and the cabbie was pointing to a multi-story building that he said Castro had built for the peasants. On the other hand, there were hardly any tourists in the hotel and half the shops on the main street were closed.

According to the cabbie, Castro had taken money from the rich people and used the money to build the building for the peasants.

Of course, it is well known that Castro actually confiscated all the wealth of the rich and successful people (shop owners among them) and then exiled them to the United States.

I remember very few people in the hotel restaurant, and when we went to the nightclub in the hotel after the ball game, the ballplayers were the only people there. There was an orchestra playing as usual, but no other customers but us.

In fact, since we were the only guys there, a few of us got up on stage and sang a few songs with the orchestra. Of course, I got up and sang a couple of songs too.

Oh yeah, I was going to tell you about my advice to Pres. Kennedy. He never did ask of course, but if he did ask my advice regarding whether or not he should approve the Bay of Pigs invasion, I would have told him "No! Don't do it."

I had seen the peasants moved from cardboard boxes in the street into new comfortable living quarters. I doubted seriously that they would have risen up against Castro when the Cuban exiles landed in the Bay of Pigs.

Kennedy was the victim of poor intelligence!

Chapter 13 Hall of Famers

Ted Williams See Chapter 1

Don Drysdale See Chapter 2

Georgie "Sparky" Anderson; See Chapter 4

Walter O'Malley; See Chapter 6

Tommy Lasorda; See Chapters 11 & 12

Sandy Koufax

The first time I walked into the Dodger clubhouse in Vero Beach was during spring training 1956. The first guy to walk over to me and introduce himself, was Sandy Koufax. A really nice, quiet guy!

And I'll never forget the first time I hit (maybe stood at the plate is more accurate) against him in an intra-squad game. Sandy had a reputation for being wild, and since there was no way I could possibly catch up with his fastball, I decided I would wait him out and hopefully get a walk. I did.

I had never seen a fastball rise that much. When the ball was about halfway to the plate it looked like the ball was going to be somewhere about the waist. When the ball reached me, it was chest high.

Another thing I remember vividly, was the sound the ball made when it passed me; another new experience. I guess when the ball is traveling over 90 miles an hour you can hear it.

Speaking of his control, or lack of it, reminds me of the time Carl Furillo was batting against him in an intra-squad game. It was very early in Sandy's career . . . 1956.

Sandy quickly got two strikes on Furillo and the next pitch was really wild. How wild?

The backstop was simply a combination of 2x4s and chain link and stood about 8 feet high. (We were on a practice field, not in Holman Stadium). Somehow Sandy's 0-2 pitch missed the backstop.

At that point the third base coach, Billy Herman, yelled "Good eye, Carl. Protect that plate."

Carl got out of the box, made an obscene gesture at Herman and stepped back in the box.

The next pitch was about eye high. Furillo deliberately swung slowly about waist high for strike three and turned around and walked back to the bench.

He happened to sit down next to me and he said "Dago, that guy's gonna kill somebody someday. But it won't be me."

In fairness to Koufax, he was probably trying to throw a curve ball . . . a pitch he hadn't begun to master. In fact, he didn't master the curve until 1961. During his first six years with the Dodgers (1955-1960), he compiled an overall 36 wins and 40 losses, with teams that were usually competing for the Pennant.

When he mastered the curve ball, he pitched the most unbelievable six-years in baseball . . . 129 wins and 47 losses;

including four no-hit, no-run games, while on his way to the Hall of Fame.

Old Timers Games

When Lasorda was managing, I was invited to the old-timer's games regularly. No, not to play in the game. Because if I were announced as a pitcher in an old-timer's game, it would sound like a bunch of owls in the stands saying "who?" After all, I was in only three games, so nobody would remember me.

No, I was invited because I could throw batting practice to the old timers before the game. It was fun!

One of those old timer's games was the Dodgers old-timers against the Hall of Fame old-timers (more on this later). I got to pitch batting practice to Henry Aaron and Joe Torre and some of the other Hall of Famers, and get an autographed ball signed by all those greats!

I'm sure Sandy was invited to all the old-timers games but he didn't always show up. I'm sure that he had other commitments. I remember very well, one of the times that he did show up.

Sandy was asked to pitch an inning and he looked up and down the bench and asked "Does anybody want to warm me up?"

I said "Yes", grabbed my glove and we went out to play catch in front of the dugout. I expected the first few throws to be soft, but then I expected him to start throwing harder. But the speed never improved.

After about a dozen or so pitches I said "I guess your elbow is bothering you so much you can't throw very hard."

He said "I can't get past the pain in my shoulder, to get to the pain in my elbow."

He went out, pitched an inning and every one of his pitches looked like it was part of a slow pitch softball game. It was very sad.

Another of the times that Sandy showed up was the 2017 old-timers game. I had arranged to sing the national anthem that day (see chapter 17) so that I'd have chance to meet and talk to all the guys that I had played with.

Sandy and Me before the 2017
Old Timers Day;
Author's collection

No, I didn't throw batting practice and in fact, there wasn't any batting practice before that old-timers game.

Of course there was a ceremony where the guys were being introduced. That included not only the guys planning to play in the game, but also people like Sandy, who was there because of the occasion and the chance to talk to the guys and reminisce about old times.

Duke Snider

I have a couple of special memories of Duke.

I was pitching in an intra-squad game at the start of Spring Training in Vero Beach, Fla., when it was the Brooklyn Dodgers and they trained in Florida, not Arizona. I got the first two hitters out (don't remember who) and Duke came up.

Duke Snider at 2008 Reunion; Author's collection

Early in the count, he dropped a bunt down the third base line. He beat it out easily, and then said to me while standing on first, "Sorry Ralph, but you've got too much stuff too early, and I'm not ready for it yet".

I thought it was a great compliment coming from him.

And then there's the time when I was pitching in a Spring Training game against the Red Sox in Miami Stadium. The outfield wall was all cinder block and about 15 feet high in center where Duke was playing.

I had two men on base with two out. The hitter drove one to deep left center, and it looked like a sure double to me, so I started running to back up home plate, because I thought there might be a play at the plate.

I looked back over my shoulder as I was running towards the plate and there was Duke running to the cinder block wall. He jammed his spikes into the wall, so he could jump higher, and caught the ball to end the inning; an amazing effort for a Spring Training game.

When I thanked him, he said, "We California guys gotta stick together."

Everyone talked about his hitting, but he was also a great outfielder.

Walt Alston

The first thing that comes to mind when you ask about Walter Alston is how even-tempered he was. He seldom displayed any temperament. He was a very quiet person.

Another thing was flashing signs from the dugout to the third base coach. He didn't go through the rigmarole that you see today on TV; touching the nose, ears, chin etc. He used different guys on the bench to flash the signs to the third base coach, who then relayed them to the hitters and runners.

So watching him didn't do any good. Also the signs used were very easy to spot e.g. right leg crossed over the left leg. Since the opposition never knew who was giving the signs, the signs could be very prominent.

Another thing that comes to mind is he was thoughtful and planned ahead.

For example, I remember one time in Spring Training, Alston walked by me and said "Mauriello you're giving the signs this inning. If the *first guy* gets on, I want the *next guy* to bunt. If the first guy makes out and the next guy gets on, I want a hit and run. Watch me. I'll let you know." Of course, he used the names of the players, but I can't remember who they were.

And Alston was a "hands on" leader. I can remember him demonstrating a hook slide to us at Vero Beach in 1956.

Roy Campanella

The first time I pitched to Roy was in an intra-squad game in Spring Training, 1956, at Holman Stadium. It was very educational.

I had two strikes on Don Zimmer and was sure that I had him set up for a change up. Roy stuck down one finger calling for a fast ball

Roy Campanella with Don Drysdale, Roger Craig, Don Newcombe, Chuck Page, and Me; Author's collection

I didn't want to shake him off because that gets the hitter thinking about something else than the one he's expecting. I decided Roy wouldn't have any trouble catching the change up even if he was looking for a fast ball.

I threw the change up, Zimmer swung and missed and I was right. Roy had no trouble catching it.

137

But he came out to the mound and said "Ralph. You shouldn't do that. You shouldn't throw an off- speed pitch when we're expecting a fast ball."

I said " Well, I was sure you could handle it, even if you weren't expecting the change up."

He very gently gave me a lecture.

He said "Ralph, with your fast ball the infielders are not expecting the hitter to pull the ball. So with a right handed hitter, they're all leaning to their left. When you throw an off-speed pitch, the hitter is likely to hit the ball to their right. If they're leaning to their left, they lose half a step, and that might be the difference between a hit and an out."

"Besides, I didn't know you had a change-up. It's a good one, so I'll work it in from now on."

I pitched to Roy several times during Spring Training but never during the regular season. Sadly when I finally had a chance to pitch for the Dodgers during the season in '58, Roy had already had that terrible accident in January of that year.

In 1986, my wife and youngest daughter, Michelle, were leaving the Dodgers office, when we ran into Roy coming into the office.

He said "Ralph Mauriello! How are you?"

I was amazed that he remembered who I was. After all I only pitched to him a couple times, and in meaningless intra-squad games.

My teen age daughter was very impressed with a father who knew the famous Roy Campanella. I told her that great catchers have great memories, and Roy was a great catcher.

Bob Feller

As a boy, my idol was Bob Feller, the great Hall of Fame pitcher for the Cleveland Indians.

Whenever I heard that he was going to pitch against the Yankees in Yankee Stadium, I went to see him pitch.

Yeah, I was a Dodgers fan, but I couldn't pass up the opportunities to see the greats in the

Bob Feller;
Courtesy of Cleveland Indians

American League. I had read and heard all about his great fast ball, but was absolutely amazed that I could see his curve ball . . . from the bleachers. It was that good.

Imagine how excited I was to find myself standing next to him, signing an autograph for a young fan in Dodger Stadium.

It happened years after I retired. It was at an Old Timer's Game at Dodger Stadium. It was the Dodgers old timers vs.

the Hall of Fame old timers. After our little three-inning Old Timers Game, we went in to the clubhouse to shower and change into street clothes.

There were sandwiches and beer and lots of talk about old times. Of course I went to Feller and told him that he was my idol and I had bought his book "How to Pitch" when I was in Jr. High school.

He said "Bullshit! I get that crap all the time."

But when I quoted some things from the book, I convinced him that I had really bought, and read the book.

As luck would have it, a few minutes later as I was leaving the clubhouse, Feller happened to be leaving as well. Outside the clubhouse door was a young man who asked us for our autograph. So that's how I got to sign an autograph on the same ball as Bob Feller.

Vin Scully

In 1956, I was a member of the Dodgers during Spring Training. We were in Holman Stadium during an exhibition game against some other major league club. Holman Stadium is a single deck with about 12-15 rows of seats, with the press box directly behind home plate at the top of the grandstand.

The dugouts at Holman Stadium are really dugouts. That is, there is no back or roof. It's just a long rectangular depression in the ground about 2 feet below field level with benches.

So we sat out in the sun while the game was going on. And the first row of seats was literally two or three feet behind the dugout, so we could hear all of the conversations going on by the fans in the grandstand behind us.

I particularly remember a quiet moment in the ball game when I was suddenly aware of the voice of Vin Scully describing the game.

I remember thinking, "Wow ! What projection. This man is over 100 feet away from me, outdoors, and I can hear him like he's sitting next to me" . . . . and then I realized that a lot of the fans behind me had transistor radios tuned in to Scully's broadcast of the game.

We've all heard and read about what a nice guy Vin Scully is. He's not only a nice guy, but he's able to do something that most of us are not able to do. Remember the name of someone to whom he's been introduced.

Vinny and Me on a night when I was singing the National Anthem; Author's collection

Once a year I sing the national anthem at Dodger Stadium, and have been doing so since 2008. Whenever I'm scheduled to sing the anthem, the first step is to go into the press box where the organ is located and rehearse with the organist.

After each rehearsal, I always wander down to Vinny's broadcast booth to say hello.

One time when I was singing, I brought with me an old friend from high school days; a man named Phil Belmonte, and of course introduced him to Vinny. Vinny and I chatted a while, reminiscing over some old times.

After we chatted for several minutes, my friend and I started out of the booth. As we left, Vinny said "Nice to see again Ralph, and nice to meet you Phil."

Just imagine! He remembered the name of my friend, who I must add has never forgotten that Vinny remembered his name. Vinny is quite a guy!

A final note on Vinny is that he interviewed me the day after my only win in the big leagues. This was before he became a legend.

After six years in baseball, I had been interviewed by lots of radio, TV and newspaper people. So he was just another guy doing an interview . . . until he started asking questions about the game I pitched the night before.

I was so impressed with his questions that I came away with the thought "Wow. This guy really understands the game. He could probably manage the club."

I sure wish I had a copy of that interview.

Other Hall of Famers

Some great hitters that I have faced include Hank Aaron who was 0 for 1 against me. He popped up to the third baseman in foul territory.

Another Hall of Famer that I had success with is Frank Robinson when he was with the Reds. It was the only spring training game that I ever started. I wound up pitching four scoreless innings. I struck out Frank twice on curveballs that bounced before they reached the catcher.

And while I'm on the subject of great hitters I faced . . . there's Mickey Mantle. He's also 0 for 1 against me . . . but only by a fraction of an inch. He popped out to short right field with one of the highest hit balls I've ever seen.

I'd say that he was about an eighth of an inch away from hitting that pitch to downtown Miami.

Carl Furillo caught the ball in short right field, and I guess he felt the same way I did, because when he came into the dugout (it was the third out of the inning) he said,

"Dago, that ball was so high, when it came down it drove me six inches into the ground."

Another Hall of Famer that I faced is Ernie Banks who was with the Chicago Cubs. This was during the season (all the other events were Spring Training). Ernie went 2 for 6 against me but I did strike him out twice.

Finally, another Hall of Famer that I faced was Roberto Clemente. He singled to center in his only at bat against me. Not a line drive, just a blooper. But just think . . . Clemente had exactly 3,000 hits in his career. Without me he would have had only 2,999.

I'm glad I could help.

Chapter 14 Umpires

Sometimes I'm asked if I was ever thrown out of a ballgame. The answer is yes; twice for sure and maybe three times . . I think. I don't remember. In each case, I wasn't pitching. I came off the bench.

When I pitched, I never argued with an umpire, because my Dad taught me that umpires are human, and if you argue with them and show them up in front of the fans, they're gonna "squeeze" you.

You're not going to get a strike call on a pitch that's close, but not quite over the plate. So when I pitched, I was a totally different person than I was when I was on the bench, which was of course three out of every four days.

When I was on the bench, all the umpires knew me and my voice. I have a very loud voice. I used it a lot yelling at the umpires when I thought they made a bad call.

Not just on calls on the bases, but also on balls and strikes calls. After all, my view from the dugout, which might be 60 or 70 feet away from where they were behind the catcher, was certainly better than their's. . . especially on balls and strikes.

Honest It Wasn't Me

The first time I was thrown out was kind of funny because I wasn't even in the game. I mean that literally. I was in the dugout, but I was not paying attention to the game.

It was my rookie year, and one of the veteran pitchers was telling a joke to me and a couple of our other rookie pitchers.

We were all huddled in the far end of the dugout about as far away from home plate (and the manager) as possible.

I was laughing at the joke when somebody in the dugout said "Hey Ralph, you've been thrown out of the game."

My reaction was that someone was pulling my leg. When I looked up there was the umpire looking down into the dugout and telling me "Morelli you're outta here." (Yeah, he mispronounced it)

I couldn't believe it and I said to him "Are you serious?"

He said slowly and emphatically. "You are gone."

I was stunned and didn't know what to do.

The veteran pitcher said to me "If he threw you out, you might as well get your money's worth. You're gonna get fined. Get out there and give him a piece your mind."

So I jumped out of the dugout and screamed at him with every swear word I knew and a few I didn't know. Then I kicked the dirt and left.

What was even funnier is what happened the next day.

Just before the start of the game, the umpire that threw me out the night before came by the dugout and said, "John you were really upset last night. Didn't you know what I was doing?" (Yeah I know my name is Ralph but he didn't. He called me John).

"I just threw out Clyde King (their manager) and the hometown fans were really on me. I figured the best way to get the fans off my back is throw somebody from your team out of the game."

"I didn't want to hurt your team, but I had to throw somebody out. You'd pitched the night before, so I knew that your manager wasn't going to use you. So you were it. You were so mad at me I couldn't believe it."

Yeah, I was embarrassed and I apologized. If I had had my head in the game, I would've realized what he was doing, and probably gone out there and said a few things, but I would've been a lot nicer in my choice of words.

He Wouldn't Ask for Help

The second time I got thrown out was very different. I not only had my head in the game, I was coaching first base. It was at Fort Worth in 1956 in the AA Texas League.

We had up at the plate a big strong left handed hitter, Jim Gentile. You might remember him. Later on he had some great years with Baltimore. (See Chapter 8)

I was not in the coach's box. I was down the right field foul line as far away from home plate as possible. Gentile hit wicked line drives down the first base line, and I wanted time to get out of the way.

Gentile hit one of those screaming line drives down the right-field line that landed about a foot fair on the grass in short right-field. The umpire was straddling the foul line, and the ball came right at him. So he dove out of the way and then jumped up and screamed "Foul Ball".

I was so amazed, I didn't scream at him. Instead I walked up to him and asked him to check with the plate umpire. I was sure the home plate umpire had seen where the ball landed. He refused to ask for help.

When I asked again and he said no, I looked at him and quietly said "I've been playing professional ball for four years and you are the most incompetent umpire I have ever seen."

I didn't wave my arms, I didn't jump up and down, I didn't kick the dirt, so I wasn't showing him up in front of the fans, I was merely voicing an opinion. He didn't like it, and he threw me out right on the spot.

Instead of screaming at him, I turned around and headed for the dugout. After about two or three steps, I stopped and turned around and said "The truth really hurts doesn't it?"

Yeah this time I did get a fine. No, I don't remember how much it cost me.

Now we solve the mystery of why I said I think I'd been thrown out three times. There was a picture in the papers of me yelling at Neil Strochia, who by the way, was one of the better umpires in the AA Southern Association. We must've had a difference of opinion.

That's me yelling at an ump; Mobile Press Register circa 1955

I don't remember the incident, but it's clear to me that I was coming off the bench, because I didn't have a hat. I always

148

took my hat off when I was in the dugout. Why? Because I read somewhere that hats were bad for your hair.

I must've been thrown out, but I don't remember.

Spring Training and the Strings

During one spring training, I ran into one of the umpires who had given me a bad time the season before. He wouldn't call a curve ball at the knees a strike. So I asked him to come with me and a catcher to the string area in one of the bull pens.

For those you who don't know what the "string area" is . . . they have two poles stuck in the ground on either side of home plate. Then they put two strings between the poles to indicate the top and bottom of the strike zone. Then they tie two strings vertically on either side of the plate to the two horizontal strings.

Got that picture? The four strings make a rectangle that defines the strike zone. It's just like the strike zone you see on TV.

It's a good way to tell whether or not you really throw a strike. If the ball is between the strings or hits the strings, then it's a strike, or should be called a strike if you're pitching in a ball game.

I took this umpire over to the string area and warmed up with my catcher, who by the way was Norm Sherry, (the older brother of Larry Sherry, for you Dodger fans). Norm wound up being a big league manager for the California Angels. But in those days he was just a minor league catcher.

I warmed up and then asked the umpire to assume the normal umpire position behind the catcher. I started throwing some curveballs. Some of those curveballs hit the bottom string and Norm, who was in his normal catching position, was catching the ball with his glove virtually touching the ground.

I said "See, those pitches are strikes."

He looked at me and said "Ralph you're absolutely right. But if I call those pitches strikes, they would run me out of baseball."

And I've got to add a couple of stories about the arrogance of umpires

He Wouldn't Ask for Help Either

It was in Fort Worth in 1956. I was pitching late in a close game with a man on second and one out. The batter hit a fly ball to center field and the guy on second decided to tag up.

I was backing up third and saw a fine throw from Don Demeter beat the runner to third base. Dick Gray was the third baseman and as he tagged the runner, the umpire called him out, and turned and ran away from the bag.

So he didn't see that Dick had dropped the ball. I could see it on the ground between his legs and hear him swearing because he didn't realize that the ump had called the runner out.

I said quietly "Dick, He called him out."

He picked up the ball and rolled towards the mound and we both trotted towards our dugout.

Of course the third base coach went crazy. He chased after the umpire screaming that the ball had been dropped and the runner should be safe. When the coach asked that he check with the other umpire, (yeah we had only two umpires in AA at that time) the umpire just simply ignored him.

This is Really Arrogance

Another story about arrogance happened in 1958 also in the Texas League. It was in ninth inning with two out and the tying run on second base. Our centerfielder, Joe Duhem was up at the plate.

I don't remember exactly what the count was, but there was one strike on Joe when he took a pitch that the ump called a strike.

Joe really got upset, and started arguing with the ump. From where I was in the dugout, I could see the pitch was high enough, because from where we are in the dugout, we get a very good view of whether balls are high or low. But of course, we can never tell if the ball is inside, outside or over the plate.

Joe made the mistake of staying in the batter's box while he turned around and argued with the umpire about the pitch. While he was arguing, the catcher threw the ball back to the pitcher. Joe kept arguing while still in the batter's box.

And while Joe was still arguing, facing the umpire, not the pitcher, the ump waved at the pitcher telling him it was OK to pitch.

From the dugout we could clearly see that the ball was about shin high. The umpire raised his right arm said "Strike three!" took off his mask and said "Now what was that you were saying Joe?"

And then he turned around and walked away because the game was over!

That's arrogance and in fact a violation all of safety rules of baseball. An umpire is supposed to protect the hitter and make sure that the pitcher never throws the ball when the hitter's not looking.

Before I close this chapter on umpires, I have to tell you that TV replay has really changed my opinion. When I played, I knew they were all blind.

But after watching all the replays, I realize these guys are very good at what they do. Sure once in a while the replay show the ump missed a close call on the bases, but they are right way more that I would have ever believed.

Chapter 15 Some Personal Stories

How I Met My Wife

I have lots of personal stories about my time in baseball but certainly the most significant personal story is how I met my wife. It was June 29, 1957, and I was with the Los Angeles Angels in the old Pacific Coast League.

I was walking out of the clubhouse with three of my teammates; shortstop Wally Lammers, catcher Bob Catton and pitcher Vito Valentinetti. And there in the parking lot, not more than 50 feet away from the clubhouse door was a green 1939 Chevrolet with the hood up, and two very pretty young ladies standing alongside.

Vito was smoking a cigar and as he saw the ladies he took the cigar out of his mouth flicked the ashes off and said in a very suggestive voice "Well . . . hello ladies."

I decided to play the role of the gallant guy helping damsels in distress. So I went up to them and said "Can I help?"

They said "We can't seem to get our car started"

Of course I thought it was strange that the car would stall right in front of the club house door. No! I didn't think that. I knew a pick up when I saw one.

So I made believe I knew a lot about cars and stuck my head under the hood and sniffed and said "Oh. It smells like it's flooded." No it didn't really smell like it was flooded, (I didn't smell gasoline) but I was sure I would have no trouble starting the car.

So as I got behind the wheel I gave a lecture about how when the engine is flooded you have to push the accelerator down to the floor, because that puts more air in the carburetor and helps fight the flooding. (I didn't know much about cars, but I knew that much).

And sure enough the car started and both of the girls were now saying "we don't know how to thank you" and of course I responded by introducing myself and found out they were sisters; Marlene and June Paulenko.

Marlene was an elementary school teacher in her first year after graduation. June was a freshman math major at UCLA.

Maybe it was the major in math that attracted me. (After all, I was studying to be an engineer at the time.) Or maybe it was the tight blue dress June was wearing.

I think it was the dress!

So I asked them if they would like to join us in a drink. Both Valentinetti and Catton were

June Paulenko became June Mauriello on January 31, 1959; Author's collection

staying at the Mayfair hotel on Seventh Street and I was going to drop them off anyway, so why not ask the girls to join us for a drink in the hotel lounge.

When the waitress took the orders of the girls, June ordered a Tom Collins. When the waitress asked for my drink, I ordered

154

a seven up and both of the girls snapped their heads around because it was a surprise. probably because the other guys had ordered regular drinks.

In the next section you'll find out that I didn't drink when I played ball. I was a slow learner I guess, because I didn't drink beer recreationally until I was thirty.

Anyway, I asked June for a date that night and she said yes.

The rest, as they say, is history. We've been married over sixty years.

Drinking Beer Medicinally

I didn't drink beer recreationally until I was 30. That means for fun. Now don't get me wrong I wasn't a teetotaler. I'm Italian, so I was raised on wine. But I never drank beer for fun, or enjoyment, until I was 30.

On the other hand, halfway through my second season, I discovered, no I didn't discover it, it was forced on me, that beer has medicinal qualities.

When I pitched, I'd sweat so much that sometimes I'd lose seven or eight pounds . . . on a hot night that is.

One night after pitching a game on a hot night in Des Moines, I was drinking water like a man who just came off the desert . . . glass after glass.

Then one of my teammate said "What the hell is wrong with you? Why don't you have a glass of beer"

I said "I don't like the taste of beer."

He said "Okay, take it like medicine. Why don't you try a beer. It'll satisfy your thirst and you won't get so bloated drinking all that water."

I shook my head and he said "You're going to college, ain't you?"

When I nodded my head he said "Don't they teach you to try things, so you can learn?"

I looked at him and I said "you know you're right! Let me try it."

And it turned out that it didn't taste so bad. So I kept drinking until suddenly it tasted terrible. And I stopped. So I guess I drank as much beer as I needed to replace the fluids that I had lost pitching the ballgame.

So I could tell how much I sweat by the amount of beer I drank. On a hot night in New Orleans, or Houston, after the ballgame I would drink two or three cans of beer. On a cold night in St. Paul, I'd have trouble getting through a half a can.

But in later life, after planting a lawn in our new house on a very hot day, I gained wisdom and drank a beer . . . or two, and I enjoyed it, and I've been enjoying beer ever since.

Shaking Off the Catcher

Every once in a while I'm asked "Who is really in charge out there, the pitcher or the catcher?" and my answer is always the same. "When I'm pitching, I'm in charge. . . unless, of course, the call is coming from the bench."

Let me tell you about an experience I had when I was pitching to Norm Sherry, a well-respected catcher. Heck, he became a manager in the big leagues.

I gave up a double to the first hitter of the inning. It was the third or fourth inning . . . in the middle of a ballgame. I got out of the inning with a strikeout and two ground balls and in the process I threw 12 or 13 pitches.

I shook off Norm on almost every pitch. After the inning, he was standing at the dugout steps waiting for me. That's because he trotted off the field; I walked off. In those days the pitcher didn't run off the mound. We felt as though it gave the impression we were afraid to be out there.

Anyway, he was standing at the steps and said "Who the #$*&@ is calling this game, you or me?"

I responded as nicely as I could "Who the #$*&@ is pitching this game, you or me? Norm, when they put winning catcher and losing catcher in the box score, you get to decide what pitches I throw. But as long as it's winning pitcher and losing pitcher in the box score, I get to decide the pitches." (Except of course if Roy Campanella is catching).

I do need to add one more thing. If the call for a certain type of pitch came from the dugout (i.e. the manager) then of course I'd throw what the manger wanted. I've had a catcher come out to the mound more than once during my career, after shaking off his sign, to tell me that the call is from the bench. I always agreed. Now I wonder if they were always telling the truth.

Illegal Pitches

I've also been asked at times, if I ever threw a spit ball. The answer is yes. But never in a ballgame!

But I do remember one time when I was in Fort Worth warming up for the start of the game, and our third baseman, was warming me up. He was doing it to give our catchers a rest. After all we only had two catchers. One was going to be in the ballgame and the other was going to be in the bullpen.

Near the end of my warmups, when I was throwing fastballs he says "Hey, Ralph, have you ever thrown a spitter?" By the way this is Marty Devlin, the same third baseman who had the tobacco chewing experience I talk about later in the book.

I answered "Yeah, but I've never thrown it in a ballgame. I've just fooled around with it on the sidelines.

He said "Really what does it do?"

I told him "It'll sink straight down and fast."

I know as you read this, you want to know how to throw a spitter. The reason it sinks is that your index and middle finger are wet and your thumb is dry. So when you throw the ball the thumb provides friction while the other two fingers are wet causing the ball slip. This creates an overspin which causes the ball to sink.

So I explained this to Marty and told him it was going to sink and to be prepared.

He said "Okay throw me one."

I did, and it hit him in the shin. He never asked me to throw a spitter again.

I never realized it, but I had a wonderful opportunity to throw a spitter anytime I wanted without being detected. When I pitched I always had a cotton handkerchief that I kept in my pocket. I would pull it out to wipe the sweat off my face and brow. After a few innings that handkerchief was really wet.

One night on a particularly hot night when the handkerchief really got wet, my catcher called time and came out to the mound and said "Damn it. Every time you take that handkerchief out of your pocket, you throw a ball. I think you're getting your fingers all wet and it's affecting your control."

I thought about it and realized that he was right. So from then on whenever I use my handkerchief, I was careful to wipe my fingers off on my uniform.

It never dawned on me while I was playing, but as I think back I realize it was a wonderful opportunity to throw a spitter. All I had to do was to make sure that the only my middle and index finger got wet and make sure my thumb was dry. The umpires knew I handkerchief in my pocket and never questioned me when I pulled it out to wiped the sweat away.

And one last thing, I had two handkerchiefs, a red one and a green one. And I had a peculiar sense of humor. As long as I was getting people out, I used the green handkerchief to wipe the sweat away. When I got a couple of men on base, I would use the red handkerchief to let the hitters know that I was going to stop the rally before it got out of hand. Did it work? Most of the time.

After all, in the different minor leagues I played in, I won 81 games and finished 72. Six of my wins were in the playoffs of the different leagues I was in.

And while we're on the subject of illegal pitches, I did throw some illegal pitches in Portland in 1957. But it was an accident. Honest. Well it started out as an accident.

I don't remember how or why, but I got some alcohol on my hands and when I went out to the mound, I picked up the rosin bag. Normally I didn't use a rosin bag, but in Portland there was so much humidity and the grass was always wet, so the rosin bag was necessary. In fact, Portland was the only place I ever used a rosin bag.

Anyway, when I picked up the resin bag, I discovered that the mix of alcohol and rosin makes your fingers very sticky. It's almost like having pine tar in your fingers. I had the best curveball of my career that night.

After a couple of innings it dawned on me that I had a foreign substance on my fingers, which is of course illegal. I do confess somewhere around the 5th or 6th inning, when it started to wear off, I put a little alcohol my hands and went out to the mound and grabbed that resin bag again. But honestly it's the only time I ever did that my career.

I was questioned one time by an umpire, in St Paul. It was about 45° when we started the game. (I didn't need a handkerchief. I wasn't sweating.) It was either the second or third batter, the umpire called time and walked out to the mound and wanted to know what I had in my pocket. I had in my pocket a hand warmer, which was about the size of a cigarette case. It had chemicals so that when you inverted the unit, it gave off heat, which was absolutely necessary in the night when it's 45°.

He gave me permission to use it and that was the end of that.

A final note about that game is during the 7th inning, as I was looking in to get my sign, snow flakes started to fall. We did finish the game, but the next day, May 1st, as we flew out of town for a road trip, the city was covered with two inches of Snow. That's right. I said May 1st.

I Wouldn't Be Intimidated

It happened in Nashville, Tennessee. I was pitching for the Mobile Bears of the AA Southern Association, and I was on a streak. I had 27 straight scoreless innings . . . three straight shutouts.

I found myself starting a game in Nashville which had a fence in right field that was only 258 feet away. The fence was 40 feet high, but it was still only 258 feet. Not even a challenge for a high school kid.

When I went on the mound for the bottom of the first inning, I turned around to look at that fence and told myself that I would not be intimidated.

The first hitter up was left-handed and I calmly told myself that I would not be intimidated. So I threw the ball down the middle and dared him to hit it. He did. A home run over that short fence and my scoreless streak was over.

161

We won the game, but I learned the hard way that if I was going to pitch in a ballpark with a short right-field fence I'd better keep the ball outside to all those left-handed hitters. They had six left hand hitters in the lineup.

Santa Barbara

When I was with the Santa Barbara Dodgers in 1953, we played in a park that was called Laguna Park. It was an old wooden structure, and I'm sure if somebody struck a match, the thing would've gone up in flames.

Although it was only Class C, we expected fans to come watch the games. San Jose and Bakersfield, who were also in the league, would draw 2,000 or 3,000 people. But at Laguna, we usually had about 400 people. In fact we called them "the faithful 400."

The park was on the south side of Santa Barbara, so it was pretty close to the ocean, and that meant that every once in a while we would have fog. Sometimes that made it exciting.

One time in the 10th inning of a close ballgame, the San Jose leftfielder, who was leading the league in RBIs, hit a line drive right at our left fielder. Unfortunately because of the fog he didn't see the ball until it was too late. There was a guy on first and two out, and he scored what turned out to be the winning run.

Yeah I remember well, because I was the pitcher. Yes I started that game. That was back in the days when the pitcher was expected to finish what he started. It certainly is a lot different now.

When I Didn't Get Anybody Out

Another story about when I was in Santa Barbara is when I was the starting pitcher and we were at home. It was just one of those nights. Everything I threw was a line drive. Six straight shots for hits. There must been have a couple of doubles in there, but I don't remember.

What I do remember was the manager, George Scherger, came out to the mound and he signaled for the catcher, Herb Olson, to join us.

George asked Herb "What's he throwing?"

And Herb said "I don't know. I haven't caught one yet."

With that, Scherger signaled to the bullpen and my pitching that night was done.

But it turns out that not all was lost. I had three friends of mine from high school who were in the stands. They had driven all the way up from North Hollywood, about 100 miles away, to watch their high school buddy pitch. Since I didn't last very long, I thought the least I could do was to entertain them.

So I took a shower, went into the stands, found them, and took them on a tour of downtown Santa Barbara. It was Fiesta night, so the streets were full, and there were lots of activities, and lots of fun.

The ballgame was on the radio and almost every other store we went in, or by, was listening, so we could keep track of the game. When it got to be about the eighth inning, I decided we needed to go back to the ballpark so I could be in the clubhouse after the game.

Another part of the same story is my father had left work and was driving up to Santa Barbara from North Hollywood to see me pitch. He managed to get the game on the radio as he was driving through Ventura, which is a town about 30 miles from Santa Barbara. When he heard that I had been knocked out of the box, he made a U-turn on Highway 101 and went back home.

What Do They Say When They Go Out to the Mound?

When people find out that I was a pitcher, I'm sometimes asked what does the catcher, or the manager, say when he comes out to visit the pitcher. Well, the answer is that it is usually about the hitter, but sometimes it's just something silly.

An example of something silly is when I was in high school, I had a catcher who, whenever he thought that I might need a little relaxation, would come out to the mound and say something like "Do you have a date Friday night?"

If I said yes, he would say "How about double dating?"

If I said no, he'd say "Get one and we can double date." That's when I would tell him to get back behind the plate and catch.

Most of the time, it's the catcher with advice, and sometimes it's the Manager with the hook.

Real Advice
One time I walked three batters in a row with 12 straight fastballs. Yeah, at times I was a little wild. The manager, Ray

Hathaway, came out and said "You can't throw the fastball over. Why in the hell don't you try something else?"

So I threw nine straight curveballs. All for strikes and I got two strikeouts and a ground ball to the second baseman.

When I got back to the dugout, Ray said "What the #$*&@ you doing out there? When I said try something else I meant for you to mix up the pitches. Not throw nine straight curveballs. Are you nuts?"

The Manager with the Hook

And then there was a time the manager, Clay Bryant, came out to the mound because I had given up a hit in a fairly critical game situation, by throwing three straight changeups.

The batter, a right handed hitter, missed the first two pitches, and then hit the third pitch off the end of the bat and hit a little blooper just over the first baseman's head for a single.

Bryant came out and said "What the #$*&@ are you thinking about?"

When I pointed out that the hitter was badly fooled and barely made contact and was very lucky to get a hit, he said "Shut up, dammit. I'm running this ball club."

And I said "Yeah, you're running it alright. Right into the ground!"

Guess what! He decided we needed a new pitcher. What could I do? I gave him the ball and walked off the mound.

What really annoyed me about the whole situation was that I had thrown two or three changeups in a row with success many times and he never complained.

I know I shouldn't have said what I did, but I was very upset.

To Clay's credit, in spite of the smart remark I made, four days later I was given the ball to start in my regular rotation spot.

Sometimes the 'Help' is Absolutely Useless.

Then there was a time in the AA Texas League when I loaded the bases with two outs and we were ahead by one run late in the game.

On one of my pitches, the batter hit a foul ball into the stands and the umpire threw out a new ball to me. I tossed it over to our third baseman, Tommy Davis. Yes, the same guy who went on to play outfield for the Dodgers and lead the league in RBIs two years in a row.

I asked him to rub it up, which is something he usually did. As he walked towards me he rubbed up the ball speaking words of encouragement and when he reached me he put the ball in my glove and said "Be smart Ralph."

Encouraging perhaps, but not too useful.

Tee Hee! I Guess You're Next

It was a dark and stormy night . . . I know what all you Snoopy fans are thinking about . . . That I'm going to try and finish Snoopy's novel. (You do read the Peanuts Comic Strip, don't you?) I won't. I have my own story to tell.

It really was a rainy night in Richmond, Virginia. It had been raining all day and it rained so hard during the day, that early in the afternoon they postponed the game that was scheduled for that night.

After dinner, I wondered what I should do that night. A couple years earlier, when I was single, I probably would've gone out looking for a girl. But since I was married, it seemed like the best thing to do was to go see a double feature at one of the local movie houses.

After the first movie, the second movie started and I couldn't shake the feeling that I had seen this movie before. I walked out into the lobby to look at the big poster advertising the movie. In small print at the bottom, it said that the movie had been previously released under a different title. Since I had seen the movie before, I decided to go back to the hotel.

I was in for a surprise when I got back to my room. Because, there sitting on my bed was an attractive young lady in nothing but panties and bra.

She smiled at me and giggled as she said "I guess you're next."

My roommate, yes we always had a roommate, was single and I guessed at what was going on. Apparently he had found a young lady who had the desire to have sexual encounters with every man on the Montreal Royals.

I picked up the phone and started calling the rooms of the single guys, because I was sure they were congregated in one room and taking turns coming down to our room to have fun with this young lady.

I was lucky because I found them in the first room that I tried. I asked my roommate what was going on, and he confirmed what I had suspected. One of the guys had met this female elevator operator who had expressed a desire to sleep with everybody on the ball club.

My roomie apologized for setting up shop, as it were, on my bed. I pointed out that she was sitting on what was now *his* bed. I asked him where I should send the young lady.

He said "Send her here. We'll figure out what to do."

So I told the young lady to get dressed and sent her on her way.

At the time I had only been married about six months, and very much aware of how rumors circulate amongst the ballplayers and the wives, and I knew this story would get back to my wife.

I decided I wanted her to hear about this firsthand from me rather than from the rumor mill. So I called her and described the situation to her and begged for forgiveness for being involved. I guess she forgave me because we're still married after over fifty years.

By the way, the title of this subsection, "Tee Hee! I Guess You're Next", was originally intended to be the title of this book and open the first chapter. But I thought it was too suggestive and probably misleading considering the material in this book. So that's why this incident is buried in the middle of the book.

The Girls in Little Rock

Since we're on the subject of girls, I've got to tell you about the girls in Little Rock. Now this is going to insult all people in Little Rock and a lot of people in Arkansas, but I swear it's a true story.

It was 1955 and I was 21 years old. I was single and every new town meant new opportunities to meet girls. The first morning we were in town, I was having breakfast with our veteran shortstop.

He had about eight or 10 years of experience in professional ball and had been in the AA Southern Association before, which is the league that Little Rock was in, so he knew the town quite well.

He looked at me and said "I'll bet you're thinking about all the pretty girls in this town and want to find one to date."

I said "Sure, why not?"

He said "Because all the girls in Little Rock are ugly."

I said" What do you mean they're all ugly? There's pretty girls in every town."

He said "Not in Little Rock."

When I started to argue with him, he cut me off and said "I'll tell you what. We're going to a movie about six blocks from here, and if you see a girl that you want to date between here and the movie house, I will buy your way into the movies."

We walked that six blocks and I bought my own ticket.

Chapter 16 Random Memories

Chewing Tobacco

I've been asked if I ever chewed tobacco. The answer is no.

But I have to tell the story about a teammate of mine who tried chewing tobacco. It was my first season and our team had five guys fresh out of high school playing their rookie year of pro baseball. Naturally one of the old timers, his name was Owen Maguire, told us all that we had to chew tobacco.

He said "If you want to be a real professional baseball player you have to learn how to chew tobacco."

It was true, in those days, that more than half of the guys chewed tobacco. Four of us politely declined, but Marty Devlin, decided to try it. He was our third baseman.

Marty was different than the rest of us because he was raised with a silver spoon in his mouth. He had very wealthy parents. I think because of that, he tried harder than most to be one of the gang. I'm guessing, but I think that's the real reason he decided to try chewing tobacco.

The night he decided to try it he was playing third base as usual and as the game progressed, he seemed to get paler and paler. By about the third inning, maybe the fourth, he ran off the field, into the dugout, and then into the runway between the dugout and the clubhouse, and vomited. Maguire, his mentor in tobacco chewing, went back into the runway to see what was wrong.

When he saw how bad Marty looked and the way he was heaving he asked "Hey! You didn't swallow that stuff did you?"

When Marty nodded his head yes, Owen said "You dumb #$*&@. You're supposed to spit that tobacco juice out, not swallow it."

I wouldn't swear to it, but I would guess that it was Marty's refined upbringing that prevented him from spitting.

Marty's experience convinced me that I probably didn't ever want to be a "real professional baseball player." No, I didn't chew gum either when I was pitching.

Following Through

When I was being taught how to pitch as a kid, I remember being told that it was very important to finish square, that is, in a position to field the ball in case it's hit back to you.

If you watch television these days, you'll see very few big-league pitchers finish square. I bring this up because of what happened at Spring Training at Dodgertown in Vero Beach.

You probably remember Larry Sherry, World Series MVP in 1959, who pitched for the Dodgers. His older brother Norm was a catcher, and as catchers are likely to do, especially when the kid brother is a pitcher, Norm wanted to coach Larry. And brothers being what they are, Larry would tell Norm to #$*&@ off.

Well this one particular day, during Spring Training in 1958, after Larry had pitched a couple of innings, Norm really bawled him out.

He said "Larry you finish with your rear end facing home plate. Damn it Larry, if you don't finish square, someday somebody's going to hit a line drive back to the box and hit you right in the ass."

I guess God must be on the side of big brothers, because it was just a few of days later that Larry was pitching and somebody hit a line drive back to the box and caught Larry flush on his rear end.

No, that's not the end of the story. This story is about the next few days in the shower after each workout. Larry had the biggest black and blue mark you ever saw, and you could see the seams of the ball. It was ugly, purple and red, and lasted for days.

We had a shower room with eight or 10 showerheads and we all showered together. No stalls. Every time Larry came into the shower room, Norm would look at Larry's rear end and say "Wow, what happened? Did that hurt? "

And Larry would say "#$*&@ you!"

It went on for days. Very funny.

Meal Money

Okay let's talk about meal money. That's what they give to the ballplayers when they're on the road. Typically the amount of money that they would give you is about what it would cost to buy a good steak in that town.

Of course the numbers are going to sound silly now, but in the 1950's if you were playing in a Class B league, with towns like Asheville, North Carolina for instance, you would get three dollars a day. On the other hand if you were in the Pacific Coast League with places like Seattle and San Francisco, you'd get six dollars a day.

And the custom was that you'd get all your meal money at the start of the road trip. For example, if you were going on a seven-day road-trip, and the meal money was six dollars a day, you'd get $42 at the start of the trip. . . . At least that was the custom.

One year I had a manager, his name was Goldie Holt, who didn't give all the meal money at the start of the trip. What he did was to dole out meal money on a daily basis.

Every morning at 10 o'clock he would sit in the lobby of the hotel, and we had to come down between 10:00 and 10:30 to collect our meal money. If you didn't come down and get your money for that day, you didn't get it. I'm sure he did this to make sure we didn't sleep all day.

But that didn't always work. We had a comedian on that team, Glenn McMinn, who decided it would be funny to come down to the lobby in his pajamas to pick up his meal money. He waltzed across the lobby, put his hand out to collect his meal money, and then turned right around and went back to the elevator up to his room.

And if you were in the big leagues, typically you'd get eight dollars a day. But, when I was playing ball, there were two major league teams that did not give meal money; the Yankees and the Dodgers.

The Dodgers stayed in first class hotels which usually had at least one coffee shop and a couple of restaurants; one might be a night club. Since we didn't get any meal money, we were told to eat our meals in the hotel.

If you ate anywhere in the hotel, including the night club, you simply signed the check with your room number. If you didn't eat in the hotel, you spent your own money. Since there were usually two or three options for a meal in the hotel, it wasn't a problem.

On the other hand, the prices in those hotels were ridiculous.

When I first joined the Dodgers in 1958, we stayed in the Warwick hotel in Philadelphia (a very classy place). One morning I had scrambled eggs (no ham or sausage), toast, coffee, and cereal with strawberries.

This was an era when you could get ham, eggs, toast AND coffee for about a buck and a quarter. . . and a bowl of cereal was a lot less than that. So imagine how surprised I was to get a bill for four dollars. I signed my name and my hotel room number. But, I felt kind of bad because I wouldn't spend my money that way.

As luck would have it, I ran across the traveling secretary, Lee Scott, in the lobby. I told him what I just spent for breakfast and how guilty I felt because of the cost.

Scotty said "Don't feel guilty! Buzzie wants the ballplayers to eat good meals. He feels that if he gives the ballplayers meal money, half of the guys will eat hamburgers and save the difference. And the other half will lose it in a card game.

Since he feels that you're only as good as the food you eat, he wants to make sure that all you guys are eating well. That's why you don't get meal money."

Buzzie's plan did stop guys from eating hamburgers, but I do remember on the plane from Chicago to Los Angeles there was a high-stakes poker game going on in the back of the plane . . . just as Buzzie expected.

Nine Lockers?

In 1959, I started the season with the Spokane Indians of the AAA Pacific Coast League and we helped the San Diego Padres open their brand new park, Westgate Park.

It was so new that nobody in the San Diego front office checked the visitor's club house. We had NINE lockers. That's right! Only nine lockers.

I guess the contractor who got the job knew nothing about baseball . . . other than a team has nine players. Our manager, Bobby Bragan, was quick to settle the arguments about who would get the lockers.

He said, "Starting line-up and me get the lockers. Pitchers and the rest of you guys can use a nail on the wall, if you can find one."

No, I don't know if the home club house had the same problem.

George Scherger

My manager in Santa Barbara in 1953 was George Scherger, who became a Coach for Sparky Anderson for many years in Cincinnati.

Sparky always said that everything he knew about baseball he learned from Scherger. And Pete Rose agreed with him because he was quoted as saying that Scherger was the "smartest baseball mind in the world."[1]

Scherger may have been real smart, but that didn't keep him from making mistakes.

One night in Santa Barbara, I was pitching in the 10th inning of a tie ballgame, with the go ahead run on second base. The next batter was leading the league in RBIs. Scherger came out to the mound and told me to walk him intentionally.

I argued that I had already struck him out three times in the ball game, and I certainly would have no trouble getting him out again.

Scherger's mistake was that he decided to let me pitch to him. The batter hit a line drive double down the left field line, and the go ahead run scored. Of course, since we were at home, we had a chance to tie it in the bottom of the tenth, but we didn't score.

I felt awful. I sat in the dugout until all the guys left the dugout. I finally decided to go to our clubhouse which was

down the left-field line. It was just a shack, so it was pretty easy for me to hear Scherger screaming and swearing in the clubhouse.

[1] Loomis, Tom (17 August 1984). "Rose at center stage with candor, charm". The Blade. p. 19.

I thought he was screaming at me for giving up the winning run, so I didn't go in. I was afraid.

Then I listened to what he was saying, and he was screaming at the #$*&@ing dumb manager who let some #$*&@ing damn rookie talk him into pitching to a hitter that he knew should have been walked.

It was probably his only mistake, but I'm sure he learned from it. But more important (to me), I was able go into of the clubhouse without fear.

Carl Erskine

The first time that Carl Erskine saw me pitch in a spring training game, he came up to me afterwards and said, "You have a really good curveball and I'll bet you have a reputation for being kind of wild."

I said "Yeah, I do."

He said "That's probably because the umps have trouble calling your curve ball. With a curve like yours, which is a lot like mine, you have to throw the ball into a teacup."

"If the catcher catches the ball thigh high, the umpire is going to say that the pitch was high. If the catcher catches the ball near the ground, the umpire is going to say the pitch was low."

"You should think about coming up with another breaking pitch that's a little easier for them to call. How about trying a slider?"

Carl was absolutely right. I had lots of trouble having my curveball called for strike. I threw directly overhand so my curveball went straight down. Not side to side or some combination of down and side to side, but straight down.

It was a big breaking curveball, so that it was possible for a curve ball to be around the knees, and actually have the catcher catch the ball with his glove

Carl Erskine signing autographs at 2008 Reunion; Author's collection

either on the ground or close to it. (See Chapter 14)

But they never would call that a strike, and oh by the way if I threw a curve ball

that the catcher caught thigh high, they would call it a ball because they said it was high. Just like Carl said.

Talking about my curve ball going straight down reminds me of the first game I pitched at Asheville, North Carolina. I had just been demoted from the Class A Pueblo Dodgers to the Class B Asheville Tourists, and I really wanted to make a good impression on my new manager, Ray Hathaway.

I went nine innings and won the ballgame, and the next day I was approached by a sports reporter of the local newspaper, and he said that I had the best changeup he had ever seen. And he'd been covering Asheville baseball for 15 years. He said he never had seen a changeup like that. It seemed to slow down on the way to the plate.

I thought this was very interesting because I didn't have a changeup at that time. All I threw was a fastball and a curve.

I was puzzled at first and I finally figured out why he thought my changeup was so great. As I mentioned earlier, my curveball went straight down. From his perspective in the press box, he couldn't see that the ball was going straight down. From his vantage point, it looked like the ball was actually slowing down

You might have to think about this a while. Maybe this is a little too technical, but you engineers will understand it.

Albie Pearson

Albie Pearson was the smallest guy I ever pitched against. The official records said he was 5 feet 6 inches tall and weighed 140 pounds, but I don't believe it. He looked smaller than that.

My first year out of high school was also Albie's first year out of high school. At that time I was playing for the Santa Barbara Dodgers in the Class C California League, and he was playing for the San Jose Red Sox. It was late in the year and it was the first time I faced Albie.

He was hitting about .330. I looked at him and thought, the pitchers are probably easing up just so they can throw strikes to this little guy. I will throw my best fastball down the middle and dare him to hit it. I did and he did. . . .a line drive right past my ear into centerfield.

Albie went on to have a successful nine-year major league career with a .270 lifetime average. In fact, he won the rookie the year award in 1958 while playing for the Washington Senators. Not bad for the guy who was billed as the smallest player in major league baseball.

Ron Fairly

It was spring training 1957. I was with the Los Angeles Angels and we were doing our spring training in Los Angeles. There weren't too many pro teams nearby for exhibition games, so we added some games with a couple of local colleges. One of those colleges was the University of Southern California (USC) Trojans, who in those days, always contended for the NCAA national championship.

It wasn't a cakewalk as you might have thought with a professional team playing a college team. In fact, I remember early in the game Ron Fairly (yeah that Ron Fairly. . . the one who played for the Dodgers for many years) came up to the plate. He took a low fastball and hammered it over the right-field fence for a home run.

As he was jogging around the bases our manager, Clay Bryant, turned around and yelled at me. "Mauriello! Pay attention, 'cause you're going to be pitching to this guy later in the game."

He was yelling at me because I was involved in a conversation with one of the other ballplayers, and that conversation wasn't about baseball.

But I yelled back "Clay, I can talk and watch the ballgame at the same time. He hit a low fastball, and I'll make sure that I keep the ball up when I pitch to him."

As Clay promised, later in the game I was on the mound pitching to Ron Fairly. Since I had seen his power, I was pitching very carefully. I threw him a high fastball. He took that fastball and hit it over the right-field fence for a home run.

As he was jogging around the bases, I couldn't help but admire him, and think "He's gonna be good someday".

I was right. He was very good for a very long time in the majors (21 years, .266, 1044 RBI, 215 HR). By the way, USC did win the game.

Rod Dedeaux

Who was Rod Dedeaux? Rod was the head baseball coach at USC for 45 years. His teams won 28 conference champion-ships and 11 NCAA national titles. I was thrilled that he wanted me to pitch for USC. As it turned out I never did. But I'm getting ahead of myself.

I first met Rod when I was a junior at North Hollywood High School and pitching for a Sunday municipal team called Trojan Lumber out in the San Fernando Valley. Although we were only supposed to play municipal teams from the Valley, somehow, one Sunday when we had a bye in the schedule, we had a practice game with the House of Murphy Trojans.

There was Stan and Hal Charnofsky, Bobby Hurtle and more whose names I've since forgotten from the USC varsity. We went 12 innings before we lost 2-0 (I pitched all 12) and I was certain that I had blown my chance to go to USC, because I had lost the game.

I was taking a drink at the water fountain behind the backstop when Rod asked me if I wanted to go to USC. Since my dad was a barber, the only way was through a scholarship, which of course Rod arranged. But not before he had a big spaghetti dinner at our home that Sunday afternoon after the game.

After I graduated high school, I played for Rod and his House of Murphy Trojans in the summer of 1952. It was to be the only time I ever had the privilege of playing for Rod.

During that summer, I signed a contract with the Brooklyn Dodgers. Naturally I assumed my scholarship had been voided. However, when I called Rod to explain why I signed (The reason was a $35,000 bonus), he told me that I had earned my scholarship on high school grades and was still entitled to it.

There's more to the story. During that fall semester of '52, the scholarship committee, which had heard of my signing, decided to cancel my scholarship, because in view of my contract, I had no need.

Rod went to the committee, without my asking, and convinced them to reverse their decision. There wasn't then, nor is there now, another coach in America with so much CLASS!

I've got to tell you one more story about Rod Dedeaux. It was in 1958 at the tail end of the season. Ron Fairly and I were among six or seven September call ups for the Dodgers.

Since we were in the second division, the management decided the young guys should play to "get their feet wet" and to see what they could do. I had the opportunity to start two games and relieve a third one. Ron Fairly was given the opportunity to play right field for a number of games.

During one of the last games that season at the Coliseum, Elmer Valo came up to me in the dugout and said "Ralph, Did you go to USC?"

When I said I had, Valo asked, "Did Fairly go to USC?"

I said "Yes"

Valo said, "I've been watching that kid play for over a week now and he hasn't made a mistake yet. USC must have one hell of a good coach."

Of course that coach was Rod Dedeaux.

Elmer Valo had a 20 year major league career as a well-respected outfielder and a lifetime .282 batting average. So praise from him was high praise indeed.

Meeting Danny Kaye

I mentioned earlier that when Tommy Lasorda was managing the Dodgers, I used to go early to the ballgame and go down on the field and talk to Tommy behind the batting cage during batting practice.

One night while we were shooting the bull behind the cage, Danny Kaye came over and started talking to Tommy. Of course, Tommy introduced me.

The first thing that I said to Mr. Kaye was that I was a great fan of his. He smiled and said "Oh thanks! Lots of people say that"

I said "I really am a fan of yours and I named a couple of his movies that I had seen. Then to convince him that I really was a fan, I sang for him a little bit of a song that he had sung in one of his movies.

I don't know why I remembered it, I just did. The lyric is absolutely nonsense. It goes something like this

"I will never forget that morning When grandpa ate the awning,
To impress a pretty young lady,
Who went for men who were shady. "

When Danny heard this, his eyes grew wide, and with a big smile, shook my hand and said "You are a fan."

Dean Martin and the Celebrity Game

While we're on the subject of the celebrities, I have to tell you I'm sure that I'm the only guy was ever booed at a celebrity baseball game; the kind of game where they bring in the stars of stage, screen and radio, as they used to say in those days, to play a couple of innings for the crowd.

When I was with the Angels in '57, we had one of those Saturday afternoon celebrity games. We had sports reporters, radio announcers, stars of radio and TV etc. and among the stars were Dean Martin and Jerry Lewis.

I had a chance to meet Dean earlier in the clubhouse when he came in yelling to our clubhouse manager that he needed a pair baseball shoes, because he forgot his. I was sitting at my locker and asked what size he wore. When he said he wore a size 10, I offered him one of my extra pairs.

185

So that gave me a chance to meet him, and since I like to sing (See Chapter 17) I had a chance to talk to him about singing. A chance to talk to a professional singer was always interesting to me.

As luck would have it, I found myself in the celebrity game pitching to Dean Martin. Naturally I wanted to throw the ball easy enough so he could get a hit. The trouble was that when I lobbed the ball as soft as I could, I couldn't throw a strike.

I wanted to throw a strike, but pitching is a rhythm and when you're lobbing the ball you have no rhythm. So it was ball one. . . ball two . . . ball three, and now the fans are screaming at me to let him hit.

So I told Dean that I couldn't throw the ball over the plate unless I put something on it. I told him I could throw soft batting practice, but it might be too hard for him to handle.

He told me he was sure he could handle it. Well. It was strike one . . . strike two . . . and strike three (he swung and missed at all three) and the crowd booed me like crazy.

Chapter 17 I Love to Sing

Let's Make a Deal

I love to sing. I'm in two choral groups and also perform thirty-minute shows for entertainment at birthday parties, anniversaries, service clubs, churches, women's clubs . . . anywhere I can sing.

When I started playing baseball as a pro, I discovered that if you went to a piano bar and sang a couple of songs, there was always a girl who was willing to let you buy her a drink. So being single, and liking girls, I did a lot of singing in piano bars. It was the best two-for-one deal around.

In 1957 I played for the Los Angeles Angels in the Pacific Coast League, and since I lived nearby in the San Fernando Valley, I was a hometown boy. Just as I always did, I would go to piano bars to sing some songs so I could meet some girls. That got me into trouble.

One afternoon midway through the season, while I was getting dressed for batting practice, I was called in the manager's office.

You may remember him, Clay Bryant. He coached third base for the Dodgers for a number of years. It was my third year pitching for Clay, so we knew each other very well.

He was my manager at Mobile in the Southern Association in 1955, and Fort Worth in the Texas League in 1956. It seemed like every spring training when the minor league managers decided who was going where, Clay asked for me.

I was really surprised when I walked into his office and he said "What the #$*&@ do you want to do for a #$*&@ing living? Sing or play baseball?"

He was like Tommy Lasorda with four letter words, only better, because he could put swear words between syllables, if he wanted to.

I was really mad. I said "Clay, how can you ask me a question like that. I've been pitching for you for three years, and you know I've always given you my best on the mound. What's this all about?"

"Last night you pitched and got bombed," he said. "After the ballgame, you're out singing at a restaurant on La Cienega Boulevard. It looks bad."

I had gone to this restaurant after the game and since they had a good piano player, I got up and sang a couple of songs. I had a date that night, so I wasn't trying to hustle up a gal.

"We won the ballgame, Clay. Am I supposed to be unhappy because I had a bad night?"

Clay said "People keep calling me up and telling me you're out there singing and drinking.

"Clay, you know I don't drink." (I drank 7-up at those piano bars.)

"I know you don't drink, Ralph. But everybody else thinks you're drinking, because sober people don't get up and start singing at piano bars. Let me make a deal with you."

"What's that?" I said.

"You live in Los Angeles and everybody in town knows you. No matter where you get up to sing, I get a telephone call telling me you must be drunk because you're standing at a piano and singing. I'm not asking, I'm telling you. You can sing anywhere you want when we're on the road. Just don't do it here in L.A!"

Since there were plenty of girls on the road, I agreed to the deal.

The Strangest Audition

These days I do more singing at ballparks than piano bars. I've been singing the national anthem at Dodger Stadium at least once a year since 2008.

It all started with my oldest daughter, Tami.

We were at a Los Angeles Lakers basketball game in 1973, and as the guy finished singing the "Star Spangled Banner," Tami, who was thirteen at the time, turned and said to me "You're a better singer than he is. Why don't you sing the national anthem here?"

"Because nobody asked me," I said.

"I'm asking," she said. "I want to see your name on the scoreboard."

I said "Okay"

And my wife, June, said "What do you mean, okay?

"Tami's right. I am a better singer. So I should get the job. I'll call for an audition."

At the time, Jack Kent Cooke, a Canadian, was the owner of the Lakers and the Los Angeles Kings ice hockey team.

In fact, Cooke was also responsible for bringing hockey to L.A. He was given a National Hockey League franchise in 1966. Cooke had also been the owner of the Toronto Maple Leafs in Class AAA International League when I was with Montreal.

Cooke's go-to guy was Eddie Paar. He hand-picked the national anthem singers. So I called and arranged an audition with him.

It was the strangest audition I have ever seen. We walked into a room where there were some benches and some audio equipment for post-game interviews, and there was a speaker overhead playing "Raindrops Keep Falling On My Head."

"Sing!" Paar said.

"Here?"

"Yes, here!"

I looked up and I said, "With that playing?"

"Yes!"

I hummed a couple of notes to myself to find the right key and started singing.

When I finished, he said "Excellent! You're just the kind of singer we're looking for. You understand that the national anthem is a march and not a ballad."

At first I thought, "Wow! This guy is a Canadian and he understands our national anthem better than most of the people you hear singing it, and most of them are American."

And, then, I found out the real reason he insisted on a straight rendition with no embellishments.

He said "Mr. Cooke doesn't want the singer to take more than one minute to sing the national anthem because he doesn't want his hockey players to get cold while they're standing around on the ice."

Then he said: "I'd like to use you, but I'm all booked for the rest of the year."

I was sure this was the classic brushoff; "Don't call us, we'll call you."

But in early March I got a call from Paar. He said "It looks like the Kings are going to make it into the Stanley Cup Playoffs, and I'd like you to sing the first game."

Then he went on to explain that he booked all his singers in the summer for the entire season. That was why he couldn't give me a job, even though he liked my singing.

So he did the next best thing. He asked me to sing at the very first Stanley Cup playoff game in the King's history. He told me that it was quite an honor.

I was excited and a little nervous. There was a big display on the scoreboard hanging over center ice that was counting the people as they came into the Forum. As the number went over 16,000, the organ started playing the intro.

As I took my breath to start singing, I was thinking, "Wow! This is the biggest audience I've ever sung for."

I had performed solos at concerts with crowds of up to a thousand people. But nothing like this.

Yeah, I love an audience.

By the way, if you want to pitch in baseball, you must like an audience. After all, you are the center of attention. And if an audience scares you, you probably will have trouble pitching.

I made it through my first national anthem without any problems. When I finished, Eddie introduced me to Mr. Cooke.

"Mauriello ... Mauriello," he said. "When I owned the Toronto Maple Leafs, Montreal had a guy by that name. Was that you?"

When I told him that it was, I remember thinking "Wow! What a memory."

I was with the Montreal Royals in the International League in 1959 and 1960. It was 1973 when this happened. So it was flattering to be remembered.

Over the next three years, I would get a call in August, and Paar would ask me to select the four dates that I wanted to sing. He hired 20 singers and assigned each singer four games. That covered the 40 home games each the Kings and the Lakers played.

Near the end of the third season, he called to tell me they were going to use a recorded version of an orchestra playing the national anthem and wanted me to sing it live one last time.

He didn't tell me why they were ending live performances, but I suspect it was because too many singers did their own version of the national anthem, and made the hockey players stand around on the ice too long.

Singing at Dodger Stadium

In 2008, Frank McCourt, who was then the owner of the Dodgers, decided to open the season with a big reunion to celebrate the Dodgers coming to LA in '58.

He brought in ex-Dodgers from all over the Country. One of the guys that came to the reunion was Carl Erskine, the team's ace in the 1950s. Carl was my mentor with the Dodgers, so we started talking about lots of things and eventually got around to talking about music.

Carl plays the harmonica and, of course, I sing.

"Ralph," Carl said, "I played the national anthem at Dodger Stadium a few years ago, and I'll bet you that if you talk to Cindy, they'll ask you to sing it." (Cindy Adler was assigned by Mr. McCourt to usher us around.)

I asked Cindy and was given a chance to sing the national anthem at Dodger Stadium during the 2008 season.

The best part of that first time was that when I got to the ballpark, they asked me if I could also sing "God Bless America" during the seventh inning stretch. The woman who was supposed to sing it, had cancelled at the last minute.

Singing at Dodger Stadium, July 29, 2008; Author's collection

When I did the national anthem before the game, the crowd was much larger than at King's games, but there were a lot of empty seats. L.A. fans are famous for coming late and leaving early.

When I did "God Bless America" in the seventh inning, all the fans had come, and they hadn't left yet either. I was thrilled to be singing for my biggest audience yet. I found out afterwards that attendance that night was 40,110 people.

During the playoffs in 2008, I got an Email from Charles Steinberg, Dodgers Vice President for marketing and public relations, saying:

Dear Ralph,

Like a manager looking down the bench for the guy who can hit a pinch-hit home run, or in your case, a hurler who can get the team out of a jam, I have a most surprising and unusual question for you. How would you like to sing the National Anthem TODAY before our 5p.m. game against the Phillies in the National League Championship Series?

I realize I risk being rude by asking the day-of, but the anthem singers whom we had asked were ultimately unable to make it, and while we do have other reserves on the bench, the idea of you—a member of the 1958 team—singing in front of these players, strikes me as very, very special.

Fondly, Charles

Unfortunately, the day in question was a Sunday that I had organized a theater party with dinner afterwards for three other couples. One of the things that my Dad taught me was, if you make a commitment, you must honor it.

I sent him a nice Email saying, Thanks, but sorry, I had previous plans. And I added "PS I'm available for any games in the playoffs or World Series", but I he never heard from him regarding my offer.

That's not the only time I was called at the last minute to replace a singer who dropped out.

In 2012, I got a call on a Friday night asking if I would be available on the following Monday. I sent an Email to all my kids telling them about it, and I was absolutely stunned that my daughter Gina, and her husband Joe, flew in from Atlanta to hear me sing. They flew in on Sunday and went home on Tuesday.

Gina said afterwards "I've heard recordings of you singing here, but I wanted to see it live."

When people hear that I have sung the national anthem at Dodger Stadium, they often ask me if it's difficult. My answer is yes.

It's not the fear of the crowd. After all, I love an audience.

No, the difficulty is the sound system at Dodger Stadium. The problem is they have a pair of giant speakers in centerfield and they ask you to stand at home plate and sing. If you're singing at home plate, the sound from those speakers comes back at you about a half or maybe three quarters of the second later.

In order to make it possible for you to sing without going crazy, they put earbuds in your ears so that you don't hear the sound coming from the speakers. Then they feed you the sound of the organ through the earbuds, so you sing to the organ as the national anthem is being played.

If the earbuds should happen to fall out while you're singing, you're in trouble. I remember Carl Erskine telling me about the time he was playing the national anthem with his harmonica when his earbuds tell out. He said he almost went crazy.

If you are near me when I sing, you get a mixture of me live, and then the delayed sound from the speakers. My daughter was standing very close to me and she said that it's very weird. Check out what it sounds like, by going to the video posted by Joseph Garcia of the Ventura County Star at

https://youtu.be/ml5u-idLnCE

The best part about singing at Dodger Stadium is the reaction of the fans. Sure, they cheer and applaud when it's over. But what's best is what they say.

"Great job, you sing it like it should be sung."

I sing "The Star-Spangled Banner" as it's written -- a march tempo with all the original notes. I don't add or change a thing.

Many singers feel they have to personalize it. Judging from comments I get, fans prefer the traditional approach over all of the "special" versions that they hear.

It's an honor to sing the national anthem, and I do it whenever and wherever I can.

Whether it's a Little League game, a Rotary Club meeting or some other event, I always agree.

It'll be a sad day when nobody asks.

Chapter 18 My Major League Experience - Off the Field

I played in the Major Leagues for one month, September 1958. But technically I was a big leaguer through the off-season between '58 and '59. It was fun. There is quite a difference in the way you are treated when you are a big leaguer.

First of all there's the food. In the minor leagues when you are on the road, you are given meal money, which is usually insufficient. Typically your meal money will buy you a steak for dinner and then the other two meals will have to come out of your pocket.

On the other hand when you're in the big leagues, with the Dodgers, there is no meal money. They simply let you sign the checks, no matter what the cost of the meal . . . as long as you eat in the hotel where the team is staying.

Most of the hotels we stayed at had two or three places to eat, including a coffee shop a restaurant and sometimes a nightclub.

Special Treatment

But the way you're treated is what's really special. For example, when we were in Chicago, since we played all day games, we had our nights off. That was before Wrigley Field installed lights.

After our first game in Chicago, we were in the clubhouse and somebody announced that we were all invited to a movie house that was showing "This is Cinerama", which at the time was the newest, latest and greatest filming technique, so it wasn't easy to get in. But somehow we got tickets . . . free of course.

The next morning I was sitting in the lobby and I guess I was looking kind of sad, because the Traveling Secretary Lee Scott came up to me and said "What's the matter Ralph? You look kind of down".

I said "I called the theater box office trying to get tickets to see "My Fair Lady", and they told me there were no tickets available tonight or tomorrow night. Ron Fairley and I wanted to go, but tickets aren't available."

Lee smiled and said "Let me see what I can do."

He came back a few minutes later and said "There'll be tickets waiting for you at the Will Call window."

That night after the game, when Ron and I went to pick up the tickets, we found out that they were not only fifth row center, but they were free.

The next night after the ball game a couple of us wanted to go to the nightclub that was on the roof of the hotel where they were doing an ice show. I called and asked for reservations and was told that there weren't any tables available for the show.

By now I had figured out how to handle things like this and I mentioned to the maitre d' that I was with the Dodgers. And somehow a table became available for three of us; Ron Fairley, Jim Gentile and myself.

200

The table wasn't bad either. It was so close that that when the ice skaters made a stop near our table, the table was sprayed with ice.

A Table Down Front

And there's more. During the winter I was a big leaguer and was treated like one. Although I was already engaged to the lady who would become my wife, I still wanted to impress her.

So I planned an evening at the Moulin Rouge night club in Hollywood. Sammy Davis Jr. was appearing and I thought it would be a lot of fun.

When we arrived at the maitre d' station, I gave my name and the maitre d' said "Mauriello, Mauriello. Are you the Mauriello with the Dodgers?"

I said "Yeah"

He said "Well we have special table for you down front".

"Down front" meant a table virtually touching the stage. That's special treatment, and he wouldn't take a tip.

June & Me in
Las Vegas for free;
Author's Collection

One of the better perks of being a big leaguer was when June and I were married.

Before the event, we were contacted by somebody in the Dodgers front office and told that if we wanted, we could go to the Hotel el Rancho Vegas in Las Vegas for four days and three nights with all expenses paid. All we had to do was allow them to take a picture of us at the hotel and allow it to be published in the Los Angeles papers.

Also I'm sure because I was a big leaguer, I was asked on a couple of occasions to be an after dinner speaker. I'm sure they haven't asked very many minor leaguers to come speak to the Rotary and other organizations.

The perks continued long after I had retired.

A Fifty-Year Reunion

In 2008, Frank McCourt who was then the owner of the Dodgers, held a reunion for all of the ballplayers who were members of the 1958 Dodgers. He flew in guys from all over the country and put us all up at the Bonaventure Hotel in downtown Los Angeles for three nights. And the wives were included!

Although I was local to Southern California, Moorpark was 50 miles from downtown LA, so I chose to stay at the Bonaventure as well.

We were treated like royalty. Two employees of the Dodgers front office were assigned to us and catered to our every whim. They arranged for a hotel suite to be open and available day and night with food and drinks all provided free.

The first night we were taken to the Coliseum where the Dodgers played the Red Sox in a game to commemorate the first game that was played at the LA Coliseum in 1958. We were introduced to the crowd before the game. We had seats on the field, right behind the home plate backstop.

Our view of the Dodgers-Red Sox commemorative game March 29, 2008; Author's collection

The next night we were invited to a cocktail party in Beverly Hills at the Beverly Hills Hotel and the Who's Who of Los Angeles was there.

On opening day of the 2008 season at Dodger Stadium, each one of the members of the '58 team was individually introduced as we walked onto the field during pregame ceremonies, wearing replicas of our old uniform. As we were introduced we went to our position.

So I joined Roger Craig, Carl Erskine and Don Newcombe on the mound along with some of the other pitchers of the '58 team. It felt great!

We were given box seats at the field level, where food and drinks were included in the price of the ticket. Of course our tickets were free. And to top it off we each were given a DVD of the ceremonies.

Finally we were told we could keep our replica jerseys, and we were also given a Dodgers warm up jacket.

I almost forgot. We were told that anytime we wanted tickets to a Dodger game, all we had to do was call Cindy Adler and she would take care of it. So if anybody wants to badmouth Frank McCourt, I will defend him because he treated the old timers with respect.

Very different than the experience I had when Fox owned the Dodgers. I called the front office and ask to BUY some good seats behind home plate.

As an ex-pitcher, I always prefer sitting there so I can watch how the pitchers work the hitters. I said I wanted to buy, not ask for free seats, and I was given the runaround. I told the people that I was a member of the Dodger alumni and I was told to call someone who handled ex-players.

When I called and asked that I be allowed to buy four good seats behind home plate, I was given doubletalk, and told that they would call me. They never did.

So that's why I'm a fan of Frank McCourt.

I was a big leaguer for only a few months, but it sure was fun.

Chapter 19 On the Field for the Dodgers

Okay, this will be a short chapter. After all, I was only in three games.

My Debut Was a Disaster

I started my big league career by walking the first guy and giving up a bloop single to centerfield to some guy named Roberto Clemente. Just one of his career 3,000 hits.

So I had first and third and nobody out.

I had no trouble striking out Dick Stuart, for the first, and only out of my debut.

By the way, Stuart had struck out four times the night before and stuck out his next time up to tie a record, at the time, for six consecutive strike outs. When they told him about it after the game, he was quoted as saying "Gee, if I had known, I would have struck out deliberately on my next at bat to get the record."

I digress. Next up was Bob Skinner, a left handed hitter, who hit a four-hop ground ball that found the hole between third and short stop. Next was another bloop single to center. It was just like the first one. It stopped rolling before the center fielder could get to it. So you see, I do mean bloopers.

Alston came out with the hook. He said "You had some tough breaks. Don't get your dobber down. I'll get you another start in a few days."

When I came into the dugout, Erskine came to me and said "Wow! You were throwing bullets out there. Remember, you don't have to throw the ball through the catcher. You just have to reach him."

He was right. I was so excited that I was trying to throw at 110%. It didn't work. I remembered those words and won my next start against the Cubs.

I Win My First One. Oops! My Only One

Of course my most memorable moment in baseball was my only big league win in Chicago with the Dodgers in 1958.

The thing I remember most was that the plate seemed wider than it had ever been during my career. I kept asking my catcher, John Roseboro, if those pitches that were being called strikes were really over the plate. He said "Absolutely".

I was amazed. "Those pitches are balls in the minors. I guess I've been pitching in the wrong league all these years".

Roseboro said "When you hit the zone that you're aiming for, the umpire will give you a wider plate, and you're hitting the zones"

Me in Wrigley Field after my only win; Author's collection

All went well until I had two down in the eighth inning. I had two strikes on Dale Long, a left handed hitter, when I bounced a curve ball through Roseboro's legs.

It would have been OK except that the runner that was on first moved to second into scoring position, and the score was 2-1 our favor.

Alston came out of the dugout like a shot and replaced me with Johnny Podres. I argued that I wanted to stay in, and Roseboro said "Skip, it was my fault. I shouldn't have let that pitch get away."

But it was no use. Podres came in threw one pitch for strike three and we were out of the inning. He pitched a perfect ninth inning, striking out the last hitter.

Roseboro brought the ball to me as a souvenir. It's now in my trophy case labeled "First Big League Win". Obviously, I expected a few more. But it was not to be.

Pitching in the Coliseum

Finally, although he was not a Hall of Famer, there's Bobby Thomson who is famous for hitting "The shot heard 'round the World". . . . the homer that beat the Dodgers in the third game of the 1951 playoff for the National League pennant.

I must finish with him, because he virtually finished my major league career.

It was the last day of the 1958 season. The Dodgers had just moved to Los Angeles that season, and we were playing in the Los Angeles Coliseum, a facility designed for football.

So they created a ballpark that was very strange. It was only 278 feet down the left-field line with a 40-foot high screen. It made for strange situations. Line drives that would go out of the ballpark in a normal field, would go into the screen.

On the other hand, high fly balls that would normally stay in the ball park, would go into the stands.

I had come in at the start of the third inning to relieve Stan Williams, whose arm had tightened up. I retired 10 men in a row and then with one out in the sixth, I walked a man, and Bobby Thompson came up.

I got two strikes on him and tried to get him to swing at a fastball that was up and in. It wasn't up OR in. He hit a very high fly ball that wouldn't have been out of Wrigley Field, but was a home run in the Coliseum. That made the score 4-3 in our favor.

After I walked the next man, I swear that Alston was out on the mound to take me out of the game before the guy reached first base. He brought in Roger Craig who held the Cubs scoreless until two outs in the top of the ninth. And then he allowed two runs, and we lost the game.

At the time I was very surprised that Alston came out that quickly. But afterwards I realized why. As it turned out, had we won that game, we would have finished in fifth place. But since we lost, the Dodgers finished the 1958 season in seventh place.

So it was understandable that Alston would want to take out a rookie when the game got close and there was so much at stake.

That was the day of the famous "blow up" of Buzzie Bavasi , the Dodgers General Manager at the time. Our clubhouse man, Charlie DiGiovanni, had set up a feast of cold cuts for sandwiches and whatever after the game.

It was set on a four feet by eight feet sheet of plywood that was sitting on top of two construction horses. Buzzie was so furious that we lost and wound up in seventh place, he grabbed one end of that "table", flipped it up and threw all the food on the floor of the clubhouse.

I did pitch for two more seasons in the minor leagues, and when I earned my degree in electrical engineering from the University of Southern California, I quit baseball and became an electrical engineer.

Chapter 20 Post Career Opportunities

I guess you can think of this as an Epilogue. Lots of books have one.

An Offer from Japan

In January 1963, I received an amazing telegram. It was an offer from a Japanese baseball team for my services during the 1963 season in the Japanese Baseball League. No, I don't remember the name of the team, but I do remember the amount of money that they offered; ¥2,800,000 yen plus expenses.

The same day that I got the telegram, I got a call from one of my old roommates, Glenn Mickens. He asked me if I had received an offer from the team that he played for in Japan the year before.

When I told him I had, he said that he had recommended me to the general manager and told him that I was certainly capable of getting people out in the Japanese League.

When I asked him about the offer, he told me that since it was ¥280 Yen to the dollar, that it was an offer for $10,000, plus expenses.

He also told me that the expenses that they offered were designed for expected expenses for a Japanese ballplayer. So I would have to spend some of my own money if I wanted to live in an American style hotel or facility such as the place where he stayed.

He said the additional amount that we would have to spend would be somewhere between $2,500 and $3,500, so I could bank the bulk of my salary. So I would have about $6,500 available at the end of the season.

But on the other hand, the Japanese at that time were not allowing cash to go out of the country. So I would have to resort to what he was doing, which was importing cameras, jewelry and any other item from Japan for friends here in the US so that he could convert his yen to dollars.

That sounded like a lot of trouble, but on the other hand it also sounded it like would be fun for me and would be an exciting opportunity for my daughter who was then three years old. Tami would learn a second language, learn another culture and, I thought, be a much better person because of it.

While that all sounded good to me, my wife, June, said "No I won't have my children being raised in a foreign country."

Since family always comes first in my book, that was the end of the issue. I sent a telegram back thanking them for the offer, but I declined.

An Offer From the Mets

In 1965, I was working on my master's degree in electrical engineering at UCLA. I knew Art Reichle, the Bruins head baseball coach, so I asked him if I could pitch batting practice to his varsity, just to keep in shape. At the time, I was pitching in a semi-pro league on Sundays and thought the extra pitching would be helpful.

One afternoon as I was walking off the mound, after pitching about 20 minutes of batting practice, I saw this New York Mets scout (I can't remember his name) and he said "Damn it! Art you SOB! That *is* Mauriello".

It seems as I was pitching batting practice, the scout became interested. Reichle thought it would be kind of funny to tell him that I was a young kid trying to get a scholarship for the following school year.

The scout walked up to me and said "My God, Ralph. What are you doing here?"

When I told him that I was an Electrical Engineer and working on my master's degree at UCLA, he said "You have better stuff than most of the guys on our big club. Are you interested in playing ball again? I can sign you to a contract for $10,000 right now and send you to New York."

Remember! This was the 1965 Mets. The 1965 New York Mets season was the 4th regular season for the Mets. They went 50-112 and finished 10th in the NL. Yes, they were desperate.

I told him "That sounds kind of interesting, but I'm making $12,000 a year right now. Why would I want to take a pay cut to play baseball?"

OK! I know you're thinking. It wouldn't be a pay cut because baseball is a six-month season. But I was negotiating . . . for fun really.

He said "I think I can get you $12,000 a year."

I said "You don't understand. I'm making $12,000 now. I would want a raise . . . say $15,000."

Now I was negotiating for real, because that sounded pretty good to me.

He said "I don't think I can get 15, but let me check it out".

A couple of days later, when I went out to pitch BP, the scout came up to me and said he could get me $12,000, but not $15,000.

I thought about it! I was 31 years old and figured that I probably had two or three more years, and it would be downhill from there. So I decided it probably wasn't worth the risk to give up my engineering career to go play baseball for a couple years.

So that's how I missed out on possibly being a member of the "Miracle Mets of '69".

By the way, that was the year when I received perhaps the best compliment I ever got. At the annual Baseball Awards Banquet at UCLA that year, I was picked as the pitcher on the All-Opponent nine. i.e. I was chosen as the toughest pitcher they faced all year.

I was pitching BP, so they always knew what was coming . . . and still they picked me. Amazing!